One Night of Regrets

One Night of Regrets

A STORY OF RESTORATION AND GRACE

BEVERLY S. HARLESS

authorHOUSE®

AuthorHouse™
1663 Liberty Drive
Bloomington, IN 47403
www.authorhouse.com
Phone: 1-800-839-8640

First published by AuthorHouse   07/29/2011

ISBN: 978-1-4634-3786-2 (sc)
ISBN: 978-1-4634-3784-8 (hc)
ISBN: 978-1-4634-3785-5 (ebk)

Library of Congress Control Number: 2011912812

Printed in the United States of America

This book is dedicated to Virginia Harless—for her courage, strength, dedication and faith which she lived by.

Shortly after deciding to write my first manuscript, this manuscript, part my family began a journey that was unexpected— the beginning of what was to become a battle for breath for my then, mother-in-law, Virginia Harless. Her lengthy stay in the hospital has afforded me the honor of spending many hours by her side. I am ashamed and embarrassed to admit that in the ten years I had been married to her son, I had never got to really know this woman I now admired so. I see it to be fitting that I am to record one of *my* deepest regrets as an intro to a book written about regrets. Although the book is fictional, the following tribute to my mother-in-law, is anything but.

I had watched my mother-in-law for over a decade care for each of her adult children with such devotion and unconditional love. As any parent has with their children, she has endured her amount of ups and downs within the relationships with all of them. Even though at times she disagreed with some of their life decisions, she has always been both supportive and encouraging to them all.

She was recovering from surgery for cancer when I met her. There have been many difficult times I have seen her endure while recovering from cancer and also through her battle with a debilitating disease of COPD.

She accepted me and my daughter, Alison, from day one into her family as if we had been born into it as one of her own.

Through everything she had gone through in the time I had been privileged to be her daughter-in-law, she showed me the meaning of love, strength and courage. More than this she showed me what dedication is. She showed me what sacrifice is.

By her actions and life she gave sight to me what it means to give your life for another's needs. I have watched her put aside the things she could have done in her life for more than four decades to care another of her sons, Keith, who from birth was diagnosed with cerebral palsy.

Not being able to speak or being able to accomplish things we take for granted, she has always provided all his needs even through her own difficult struggles. I cannot say that she was unable to do the things she wanted to do, because she would not want to do anything other than be there for her son—regardless of the magnitude of sacrifice required.

At the moment in time I am writing these words, we know that the time we have left to spend with her is limited. God is calling her home. I could try to put into words my feelings of loss that I will feel when she is no longer in our presence, but there are no words I could use to describe that loss.

However, my heart is full of joy and praise that our most gracious God allowed me to share a part of my life with such woman who has so deeply touched my heart. I am also extremely thankful that he made another wonderful woman to follow through on the commitment my mother-in-law had in caring for Keith. This woman is Keith's sister, Carol. She is already to be commended for the dedication she has always shown in caring for both her mother and Keith.

She, too, is as dear to me as my Virginia. I am proud to say that both of these women who I admire so much, will always be a part of my family.

Virginia Alice Harless passed away before she could read this manuscript which she encouraged me pursue before it was finished.
September 7, 1931—August 4, 2010 (The beginning of life more abundant)

During the last days of Virginia's life on this earth, Keith became very sick. He was hospitalized shortly after his mother passed away. He was able to come home to Carol's on his 46th birthday with hospice care. Keith passed away the next day, August 30, 2010. He is now once again with the mother who gave all that she had for him.

Chapter 1

The night air was pleasant. This was a welcomed break from the exhausting heat that Becca had endured the past few weeks. She took a deep breath as her whole body relaxed. It seemed as though she couldn't remember the last time her lungs had been filled with air that didn't raise her temperature to the point of almost being unbearable.

It was unusually quite in the small town where she lived. She loved it there. She loved the quaint community and being able to walk down the narrow sidewalks and neighbors wave to her from their porches as they drank iced tea as she was passing by. It seemed as though Alfred, the local postman and everyone's personal confidant, was always looking over his shoulder for the neighborhood canine bully. He took quick, giant steps while poised to swing the heavy, blue bag harnessed over his shoulder as he entered each yard to deliver packages and envelopes.

Becca could certainly understand why Alfred kept his guard up for less than friendly dogs. He was short and kind of round. She couldn't imagine that he could run very fast. But, every time she saw him cautiously walking up someone's sidewalk, she wondered to herself, "The town is so small. He must already know the houses where all the vicious dogs belong." She would just shake her head and grin, being amused at the thought.

The same retired gentlemen standing outside the only convenient store in town always seemed curious to her. Their conversation was always the same, at least since the short amount of time she had lived there. They always were discussing politics, locally and national.

At times, it seemed as if the conversation may turn into fist blows. Somehow emotions always calmed just when it seemed as though things were about to get out of hand. Then out of the blue, someone would change the subject to the vegetables that were for sale at the local farmer's market, near the train depot, the Saturday before. She respected the manner in which they all seemed to know when to draw back when things got tense. They mainly said their peace about what they believed then withdrew without persisting. She sensed it was to keep from causing hard feelings from others in the conversation from developing. "This is an admirable trait", she thought to herself. This was not an attitude she was accustomed to.

She did appreciate that whatever the conversation of the morning was for the gentlemen, how they always stopped, and at least briefly asked everyone as they came in and out of the store how their day was.

Even though she had only been there a few times in the morning, that politeness extended to her as well. Mr. Bennett would tip his baseball cap to her and smile. Mr. Jackson would simply say, "Good morning". She always replied back the same to him. Mr. Jackson made her grin each time because it seemed as he greeted her, he could never look her in the face as he seemed to blush as she approached the store. She thought it odd that Mr. Bennett joined in with the other men. He was so much younger.

Mr. Jackson's son, Jacob, however always followed her inside and tried to go unnoticed as he stayed a half an aisle behind her until she went to the counter to pay for her things. She always bought a piece of candy and handed it to him before she walked out the door. She couldn't help herself. He had sandy blonde hair, deep brown eyes and a smile that could light up the whole town. There was no doubt about it. He was going to be a heartbreaker some day.

The other men, Becca didn't know well enough to know their names, but they were always smiling as she neared them as well.

She was still getting accustomed to going to the post office or drug store and finding a plain piece of notebook paper taped to the door that read, "Will be back soon. Ya'll can call me at my house if need be". Everyone knew everyone else in this small town, she thought to herself. It was as though time had stopped and was standing still in this new town she now called home.

The days since she had moved to this small town were somewhat uneventful. Each morning she would fix herself breakfast; usually bacon and eggs with toast loaded with grape jelly.

She didn't understand the whole "experience", as town people called it of grits. She wondered to herself, how could anyone swallow something with little flavor and the consistency of sand particles. She knew butter made things taste better but not so much in the case of grits.

She would then run to the store to pick up the local newspaper which consisted of local events, church socials, births, deaths, anniversaries, and a few postings in help wanted section. She would circle any possibility she could find and start out with newspaper in hand to apply, hoping to find something to give her income before the end of the day.

This particular day was no different than any other day. She had started out with aspirations of being able to pay her phone, electric and rent before running out of the savings she had managed to hang onto while living in the city. At least she had managed to learn the value of making her dollars stretch as far as they could possibly stretch. It was difficult going from day to day and only getting what was necessary. She would not go into a store unless she needed something and didn't let her eyes wander—keeping them focused only on what she had went to get, as if she had blinders on.

She was hopeful that the small re-sale clothing store would call her for the manager position she had applied for a few days before. She was certain this was a job she could do even though she had never managed anything well in her life, including her own life. This was according to others she knew.

"How hard could it be?" she thought to herself. Sorting through bags of used clothing, steam ironing and hanging them on the racks throughout the store couldn't be rocket science.

After that she would just have to wait for someone to come in and pay for what they had picked out.

Nope, there had to be a lot more to it than just that. She had to remind herself that others had pointed out to her one of her faults was not thinking things through. This fault, she was told, made things sound simple and lead to her jump in head first only to find out later that things are always more complicated than she thought.

She just might have to run this through her mind some more instead of just assuming this was what she wanted to do. At this point in her life, she couldn't turn down even a job she didn't want to do. "No more thought needed. I have to take it if they offer it to me. It's either that or don't eat."

After returning home she always managed to go through her daily pile of mail which mainly consisted of junk mail and a few bills. She separated each envelope she opened into three categories; one for trash, one for bills to pay and one for bills to pay later. At times she longed for a separate category for letters from friends and family. But since she had left the city without letting anyone know her whereabouts, she would quickly turn her mind to cooking dinner. Her pantry wasn't very full on any given day, but somehow she would manage to prepare something pleasing to her taste.

Occasionally she would pick up her stationary and write a letter to a close friend or family member. But, that was as far as it went. She never picked up the envelope to address it, let alone get to the post office to mail it. Somehow she just could not bring herself to contact anyone. She knew there were people that were worried about her and wanted to know how she was doing. It just wasn't enough for her to follow through with sending her letters.

One of Becca's neighbors, Mrs. Kirby, an elderly lady who was in bad health and suffered from a heart condition had visited upon her moving into the neighborhood. She had greeted Becca with country fried steak, which she had thought was rather good, corn on the cob which was smothered in butter, butter beans and cornbread.

Becca had asked Mrs. Kirby for the recipe for what she thought was the best part of the meal she had brought by on the previous Sunday which consisted of green beans and some sort of crispy onion smothered in an unknown broth. Of course Mrs. Kirby was absolutely delighted to help her out but was horribly shocked to know that a woman of Becca's age had never had green bean casserole before.

Mrs. Kirby was well into her 70's with absolutely beautiful, soft, wavy grey hair. She had the softest blue eyes that made Becca believe she was able to look into her very soul when they talked. She wondered if Mrs. Kirby could see her entire life filled with mistakes as they gazed into each others eyes every time they met.

Becca imagined her soft flowing hair she had piled into a bun being stunning when she let it down to brush it at the end of the day. Mrs. Kirby was small in stature, but Becca just knew that the size of her heart was enormous. She knew that she had found someone she could call her friend and could allow herself to get to know as well as letting Mrs. Kirby get to know her. She was certain Mrs. Kirby would never use any of their conversations against her to cause hurt to her in the end. There was just something genuine and sincere about her. She could tell her values and morals would never allow her to act in a way that wasn't from the sincerest of heart. She felt safe when talking to her.

This particular evening, Becca fixed dinner which included Mrs. Kirby's green bean casserole then sat on her porch. She was rather proud of herself for being able to follow the directions Mrs. Kirby had given her for her new found favorite side dish. She was extremely full, especially after ending up her meal with a bowl of homemade banana ice cream which Mrs. Kirby had rushed by earlier that day for her to try.

Becca longed for someone to share her evenings with. Often times she imagined herself as a wife and mother. She thought how it would be helping do homework, cheering at soccer games, and glowing with pride while attending a piano recital.

She imagined being able to let go of the fear she harbored of letting anyone get close enough—just long enough to allow someone to sweep her off her feet.

She knew this would never happen. Over the years it had been branded into her heart and mind that because of how she was, she would never deserve to find anyone who would appreciate her.

At the thought of this, her face grew red with anger, resentment and hostility not only for the one who had beaten her down to a shell of her former self, but also at herself for allowing *him* to do it.

Becca cleared her mind to the present time and decided to leave the past behind, at least for the moment at hand.

Becca was now looking forward to the possibility of getting a well needed sleep. With being completely full and satisfied from dinner, she couldn't imagine anything stopping her from falling right to sleep, not even the heat. She was certain that finally she could rest the entire night with the cool breeze of her fan rippling the sheet which draped over her while she slept. She was anxious for the installation of an air conditioner she had purchased for the older home she had moved into. It would be a welcome addition in her bedroom. The heat of the day was bearable, but the long muggy nights in Eastern North Carolina were miserable.

She tried to concentrate on the following day on what her next move would be as far as trying to find a job. She thought it may suit her to try finding a part time job in the neighboring town which was just a few miles away. It was a slightly larger town and more possibilities of at least finding something part-time. Maybe they would have a little more to offer.

It was nearing dusk when she noticed the Callahan's coming outside with what she assumed to be their great grandchildren. She had never seen children there before. She assumed their family had come to visit for the weekend. She smiled while watching the youngest boy of three trying to throw a football with the same smooth spiral his older brothers were throwing with. The Callahan's were beaming with pride and love as they watched the boys play.

Occasionally Mr. Callahan would call out to the older boys to help coach their smaller brother in the rules of the game. She could hear his telling them with a gentle voice, "Alright boys, you were smaller once too. It's your job to guide and teach your younger brother and show him the ropes".

The older boys settled down and the oldest, who looked to be about twelve, went to instruct his younger brother of about seven. He showed the younger boy where to place his fingers on the ball with such patience. After several attempts at throwing the ball, he achieved a nice spiral just as the older boys had thrown. Finally Mrs. Callahan called the boys inside to wash up for the after dinner snack she had prepared for them, but the boys dismissed her call until she yelled.

"Homemade chocolate chip cookies and don't forget to wash your hands or no cookies!"

"That sure did the trick", Becca said to herself out loud as the three boys quickly ran inside, leaving the football behind.

The Callahan's were just about the cutest couple she had ever seen. She assumed they were in their eighties. Mrs. Callahan was always dressed in a linen dress, sometimes solid colors and sometimes prints, some of the most beautiful prints Becca had ever seen. She always wore a broach that Mr. Callahan had gotten for her as his wedding gift they day they were married. Her back was slightly bent to one side but you had to look close to notice. She walked with a cane which caused her to walk a little slower and with more caution than Mr. Callahan. Her glasses fit lower on her nose than most and when she was serious about something or was trying to make a point, she would look over the rim when she spoke.

She thought Mr. Callahan was very handsome for a man of his age. He was rather tall and slender, but not too slender. He was in excellent health. It wasn't hard to tell he had really taken care of himself. Becca thought maybe a little coloring was used on his hair and that maybe he was an athlete in his younger years. She could tell that he adored Mrs. Callahan. He always opened the car door for her and was always holding her arm whenever they walked down the street, just in case Mrs. Callahan stumbled. Yes, they were indeed the cutest couple she had ever seen.

Becca's mind drifted back to the man in her past. She was fighting the desire to contact h*im*. But she knew it was for her own good to stay as far away from him as possible.

The whole reason for moving to a small town was to see if she had a shred left of anything that she once was.

If she contacted him, he would only draw her back into making her feel responsible for his happiness.

She was no longer in the position of being criticized for everything she said or did, to avoid an emotional outrage or break down from *him*. And she wanted to keep it that way.

It had gotten to the point of being more than she could bare. She would never be put in that position again.

Quickly Becca turned her mind toward tomorrow.

Her thoughts about tomorrow's plans kept getting pushed aside as she reflected on what she had witnessed the past two Sunday's. She had slept late, as she always did on Sunday mornings, until about eight thirty or so. She had planted herself in the rocker on her front porch after waking up and sipped her coffee. Then she watched her neighbors prepare for their ritual, as she decided she would call it, while she continued to sip her coffee and glance over the paper which was left on her front steps. She knew she would do the same thing again on the following Sunday, since most stores didn't open in her town until after one o'clock and she would not answer an ad for work until church had let out and the stores opened for the day. She had made this *her* Sunday ritual.

She couldn't get it out of her head—the town's people Sunday ritual. Becca said to herself, almost in a whisper as if she were afraid someone would hear what she was saying, "This is extremely irritating. Why is the goings on in this town on Sunday mornings taxing my head this way?" No matter how she tried pushing this thought away, she kept coming back to watching families as they jumped into their cars, dressed up and smiling. Kid's saying as the exited their porch, "Hurry up Dad. We'll be late for Sunday School *again*". They seemed so anxious, as if it was the highlight of their week or something. The adults and children all carried their Bibles and notepads with them as they eagerly got into their cars. Even though these thoughts were irritating her, she grinned when thinking about Mrs. Kirby coming down the sidewalk walking with her Bible in tow, talking and laughing with the Callahan's who walked along side Mrs. Kirby on their way to church.

Becca's mind went back to *him*. If only things could have been as happy when *they* were together as it seemed the Kirby's were. If only he could have controlled his own emotions, maybe then, she could have controlled her own as well. She never wanted that kind of power over his emotions. She only wanted his heart.

Becca switched her thoughts back to Mrs. Kirby and wondered if . . . . No she knew in her heart that Mrs. Kirby was the kind of person she was as a result of not only going to church but also being a doer of what was taught in church. She would however never admit what she knew in her heart to another living soul. No one she knew in the city, or at least anyone she had been close to would have appreciated the cause for the remarkable way Mrs. Kirby had for making everyone feel important.

Becca longed to find the peace she witnessed from Mrs. Kirby and the Callahan's. She wasn't convinced completely what contributed to their contentment. Deep down Becca longed to have it, too. She had tried to find that contentment and calm within herself but couldn't quite put her finger on the reason it seemed out of reach. She had never found it in her younger years of going to church. She was sure that somehow something was missing. She had been the master of her fate. She had controlled her emotions and analyzed everything before making a decision, at least in the only way she knew to analyze them. No matter what the situation, she had always done things according to her own best interests and in a way that was right in her own mind.

She was in control. Why then did she feel so empty? She once again pushed these thoughts away in desperation to escape them. She decided to put an end to these silly questions she was asking herself. Becca was yawning as she made her way to her bedroom. Muffled by a yawn she expressed her plan out loud as if saying it would have power over what she wanted to forget, "Sleep. That's what I need. Maybe then I can turn my brain off and cast all these dreadful cares away".

She climbed into her bed after turning the table fan where it would directly hit her as she slept. She sighed and thought to herself again how wonderful a full night of sleep without all the sirens, party goers, people yelling and rail cars disrupting her sleep as it had for years in the city. She was sure the debilitating heat wave had been the reason she hadn't gotten a solid night of sleep since leaving the city.

Becca struggled to fall asleep. She glanced at her clock. It was only 9:00 pm when she had gone to bed. Again she was wide awake. Something was gnawing at her. She tried once again to go to sleep but to no avail. She was *still* awake. The clock had only moved a few short minutes since she had last checked the time. She was being kept awake by things she hadn't thought about in years. She tried to shut her brain off again and again, but these thoughts were *so* persistent, no matter how hard she tried to suppress them, they just kept coming back. After what seemed to be an eternity of tossing and turning, she cried out in a loud voice, "Alright, you win!"

She knew at that moment the only way to get rid of all the clutter in her mind was to confront all the thoughts she had so successfully been able to keep buried deep inside for so long.

There was nothing left to do except let all the things bottled up inside of her rise to the surface.

Becca let her mind go to finally let in all the voices she had not wanted to hear, beginning in her childhood.

Chapter 2

"Becca, you have to treat others with compassion and take their feelings into consideration. You can't just look at someone and decide if they should be your friend because you like or dislike the way they look".

It was as if her grandmother was sitting on the side of the bed as she had been when she was six years old. The feelings of being punished by her grandmother for making fun of the new girl were as present as they were that day.

"But, grandma, she looks different than me. She dresses different than me. Her hair is different than mine and . . . grandma she doesn't even talk the same as me. She's so proper, and everyone just falls all over her like butter on hot potatoes. What makes her so much better than me? After all this is my birthday and it was my party. Everyone should have been falling all over me—not her", Becca replied filled with jealousy.

Stephie had long blonde, flowing hair. The curls laid perfectly around her face framing it as if it did so naturally. Her cheeks were rosy red, just slightly lighter than her lips. Her blue eyes danced when she laughed. She knew all the manners Becca's father had tried to teach her.

Everything that came out of her mouth was perfect—no whining or complaining or begging for everything she saw that she wanted. Completely opposite from herself and it infuriated Becca how Stephie seemed to be so perfect.

Becca had met Stephie just one week before. The ladies from church had gone over with baked goods of every kind to welcome the new family and to introduce themselves. The ladies talked with Stephie's mother, Mrs. Gilbert, while Stephie and Becca when to Stephie's room.

Stephie had everything—A television, a stereo, a closet full of clothes, posters on the walls, a white canopy bed that had a step beside of it because it was higher than the normal bed.

Astonishment filled Becca as she took in the room. Within moments her astonishment turned to envy when realizing the yellow and white lace bed coverings were the same ones she had begged her father for, but did not get.

Envy turned to rage when the two girls went outside and Becca saw the very bike she had been wishing for leaning against the back wall of the house. After returning inside, Becca's grandmother turned to Stephie as they entered the kitchen to get a snack.

"Stephie, your mother says you are taking piano lessons and you play rather well. When you finish your snack, could you play something for us?"

It was obvious to Becca that Stephie had put a lot of practice in playing the piano. But, they were both so young, she couldn't imagine being able to do anything like that herself.

After their snack, Stephie played Bach on the piano. All the ladies raved over how well she did. Needless to say, Becca wasn't excited or impressed with Stephie's performance.

Stephie seemed to have everything. The one thing Stephie had that caused Becca more pain than anything was that Stephie had a mother.

Becca could still feel how much she disliked the new girl even after all this time. She could feel her face tightening up and the edges of her mouth curving down. Her eyes were squinting with intense anger as it was building up inside of her. She remembered being treated unfairly on such a special day.

Once again she could almost feel her grandmother's breath on her neck as she recalled her grandmother leaning down to kiss her cheek and whispering in her ear, "Becca, always remember and never forget to do unto others as you would have them do unto you." Becca, remembered thinking to herself, "Yeah, right. I should do unto her the way she did unto me. If that's the case, next time this new girl will won't get more attention than I do—no matter what I have to do to make sure everyone's attention stays on me. What kind of name is Stephie anyway?"

She had always tried to outdo everything Stephie did. Most of the time she was trying so hard to outdo her, she ended up with egg on her face and finding even her friends shaking their heads at her shenanigans to outdo Stephie. This only made her filled with more distain for Stephie. It made Becca feel more and more like a failure.

For just an instant Becca asked herself a question, "Why?" She answered her own question in her next thoughts. "Actually Stephie liked all the same things I did. We were always at the same movies, Stephie was always playing the same songs on her record player as I was when we were growing up. Even though it made me furious at Stephie, for the most part we always seemed to buy the same t-shirts, jeans, and even swimming suits as teenagers." Then Becca's mind switched to another place and time.

Becca remembered getting up very early one morning and getting ready for school. The first thing that popped into her mind had been, "Everyone will dote all over Stephie today. It is her sixteenth birthday. I can't even beat her at getting my driver's license first. Why does *she* have to be a year older than I am?"

Her father stopped her as she was coming down the stairs after she finished getting ready for school. She could tell something was seriously wrong. She remembered her father saying to her, "Becca, don't leave for school right now. I would rather you go back up to your room for a bit".

Becca pushed past her father with an intense curiosity about what was going on. She stopped in her tracks when she saw the white pickup truck turned side way in the street in front of *their* doorway. She was horrified at the sight of *so* much blood trailing behind where the truck had stopped. She walked down her sidewalk with her father following behind pulling at her when she saw the white sheet draped over someone who had been hit by the truck. A puddle of blood had stained the sheet. Becca gagged from the sight and began to cry. She couldn't speak to ask what had happened. She could hear her father's voice as he whispered to her, "Becca, if you don't want to go across the street to Stephie's house to ask her parents if there is anything we can do for the family, you don't have to". Becca replied slowly, "No Dad. I want to go with you". She was in shock, still not knowing what had taken place. The sound of sirens filled the air.

As Becca and her father entered the front door, Stephie's mother was sitting on the floor sobbing, trying to keep her composure. Stephie's father was sitting beside her whispering, "I know honey. I know." Becca's Dad knelt down and spoke softly with so much kindness then motioned for her to move toward the door to go.

As they were opening the door to leave, a tearful faint voice stopped them. "Wait just a second before you leave. Stephie would want you to have this, Becca. She was on her way to your house when the truck came out of nowhere and . . . ." Stephie's mother could not hold back her tears, but managed to hand an envelope to Becca. "Thank you", Becca said quietly, not knowing what Stephie would have wanted to give her. Stephie's father added as they left the porch, "Becca, Stephie always really liked you".

As Becca and her father crossed the street, they passed the pickup truck once more. The sirens were now silent. Two emergency medics were closing the back doors of the ambulance where they had moved Stephie's body to.

Her father tugged at her arm to hurry her away from the horrific scene.

Once inside their house, Becca's father went to make a few phone calls to others with the news of Stephie. Becca waited until he was in deep conversation to exit the room.

Watching from the front porch where the scene played out of Stephie's horrible accident, the spot where Stephie had laid was cleaned—at least somewhat. The ambulance pulled off with only its lights flashing. All that remained was a police car, the pickup truck and two police officers talking to an older man along with a teenage boy.

The older man's eyes were full of tears as the policemen escorted him and the boy to their patrol car. As they were getting into the car, the younger man paused and looked Becca dead in her eyes. She perceived no fear or remorse over what had taken place on the face of a stranger she had never seen before. Chills ran through her whole body as she turned to go inside.

Becca walked through their door and slowly walked upstairs to her room where just a few minutes earlier her distaste for Stephie began her day. Becca slowly opened the envelope and unfolded the paper inside. Becca began to read:

Becca,

I know we have never been close. I am sincerely sorry for that. We are getting older now and I think it would be wonderful if somehow we could put all that "stuff" aside and really work on getting to know each other. I know you are upset that I am getting my license before you. But, I think it would be cool if we could shop together and catch a movie from time to time. I am just slightly older than you so I promise I will look out for you and be a good friend, if only you give me the chance. It's only two more years before I am eighteen and we will probably go in different directions with our lives. I would hate to miss out on a friendship if one is possible. One day it may be too late. Give me a call later and at least let me know what you think.

Hopefully Your Friend,
Stephie

Becca folded the paper and placed it back into the envelope. She was sitting on the bed when her Dad knocked at her door and asked her if she would like to stay home that day. She nodded and sat silently while clinching the envelope.

"How could I have let all those years go by?" she whispered in the dark. She had no option but to let all the feelings she had buried so deep, for so long, surface. She felt her heart sink deep into her chest as she began to remember all the things she really admired about Stephie. So many memories flooded her mind.

She had been sitting on her front porch just a few days following her sixth birthday. She had been so excited about getting the bicycle she had pitched such a fit over getting while in the store looking at it with her Dad just a few days before she was to turn six. She was desperate to have it. When her Dad told her she would have to wait and couldn't get it that day, Becca began to yell and stomp her feet right there in the store. She cried while yelling at her Dad, "How can you be so unfair to me? You don't love me because you won't buy me this bike *RIGHT NOW!*"

Becca had been so wrapped up in her temper tantrum she was unaware of everyone in the store stopping what they were doing and looking to see what the commotion was about. She hadn't noticed the other parents staring at her Dad shaking their heads with disapproval. The clerk had even raised his eyebrows, tilted his head and walked away from the two. Becca's Dad had no choice but to pick her up, toss her over his shoulder and exit the store.

The entire ride home she cried and refused to look at her Dad. She just knew that if she behaved badly enough and for long enough her Dad would turn the car around and head right back to the store in order to gain her approval of him. Instead he kept driving the car forward until they reach their street, made a left turn, and proceeded home. She was infuriated with her Dad and made up her mind she would never forgive him for denying her of what she had wanted.

"Couldn't he tell how badly I wanted that bike? Maybe I didn't yell loud enough to get him to understand that I must have it", Becca said to herself after returning home as she headed up the stairs to her room.

It was as if a scene from a play, her consciousness faded into darkness. But, it wasn't long before the curtain began to rise in her mind once again.

As she sat on her porch her eyes were swelling up with tears and she starred at the bike she had parked at the bottom of the porch steps. This time her tears were not from anger but from sadness. She had no one to ride her bike with. She was filled with disappointment when several of her friends had refused to let her ride to the park with them after she had been bragging about her new bike.

Becca noticed Stephie coming outside from across the street. Quickly she wiped the tears away and walked down the stairs to her bike as Stephie made her way on her bike across the road. Stephie rode down the sidewalk and spoke to Becca, "Hey Becca, want to ride to the park with me and play for awhile?"

Becca took another look at Stephie's bike, noticing it was just like hers and replied, "Nope, I'm waiting for my friends to come outside so I can go with them". She was shocked when Stephie spoke up and said, "Fine. Talk to 'ya later. Let me know if you change your mind. By the way, we have the coolest bikes in town", and began to paddle her way toward the park.

Becca spent the rest of the morning waiting for her friends to come by her house. Finally Becca had given up on anyone coming by. She knew they were all having too much fun at the park playing on the merry-to-round, swings and slide to come back home before lunch. Becca gave up waiting and parked her bike in the garage to go inside to watch television the remainder of the day.

Just before it began to turn dark outside, Becca and her Dad were sitting on the porch swing when Becca noticed a herd of bicycles heading toward her house from the park. They all peddled past her house without saying a word, all except for Stephie as she had stopped at the end of their sidewalk to wait for a car to pass before crossing the road to go home. But, as she was waiting she turned her head to say to Becca, "If you want to ride with me to the park tomorrow so we can play, just let me know. I'd like that."

Becca's Dad told her he thought it would be a great idea if she rode with Stephie the next day, and asked her to think about it. Becca just shook her head and went inside.

Becca realized she had dozed off as she rolled over and began having thoughts of the middle school bully she had known in sixth grade. It was as if she were half awake yet half asleep.

She lay there motionless as she re-lived sitting in the girl's bathroom sobbing. She had ran to escape after being humiliated by a girl named Chloe in the lunch room moments before.

Chloe lived in the biggest house in the neighborhood. It seemed that she had everything a pre-teen could ever ask for—and she had no problem letting everyone know it. She told everyone every time she got something new. To Becca, Chloe was almost, if not more perfect than Stephie. Chloe took ballet classes, piano classes, was captain of the cheerleading squad and had little interest in being friends with anyone that was not as refined as she was.

This particular day, Becca remember feeling more like a failure than she ever had. She had written a note at the beginning of lunch to Matt, and asked Todd to give it to him while in the lunch line.

Matt was the politest boy she had ever met. She couldn't stop starring at him. His dark, brown hair lay close to his neck line just above his shirt collar in soft waves. His smile made everything seem so much better to Becca, even on the worst of days. He had spoken to Becca almost every day since school began that year. Each morning Becca had made an extra effort to style her hair. She learned how to use make up and pick out just the right fragrance of body spray, in hopes that Matt would talk to her again that day. It didn't matter what else anyone said or did to her. All that mattered was that Matt would notice her. She was filled with expectations of receiving a compliment about her hair as he had done earlier in the year.

Becca trusted Todd not to tell anyone about the note she had written to Matt. Todd had always kept his word when someone asked him to keep something confidential. She knew even if he was threatened physically he would not break a promise. Becca had often thought to herself that it would be interesting to be Todd. He knew everything about everyone yet he managed to keep all those secrets and details to himself.

Just as Todd approached Matt's table and reached out his had to deliver Becca's note, Chloe appeared out of nowhere and grabbed the note from Todd's hand and began to read it out loud so everyone could hear. Once Chloe had finished reading the note she turned and announced to everyone, "Matt, like Becca? Matt has better taste than that." Chloe began to laugh loudly as everyone joined in with her.

Becca was crushed. She wished she could magically disappear. She ran to the other end of the lunch room and flew out into the hallway and headed to the girl's bathroom. She was sitting on the floor, in a corner, beside the sink when Stephie walked in and softly questioned, "Becca, are you in here?" Becca keeping silent, just sat there not responding and holding back her sobs in hopes Stephie wouldn't hear her.

Becca heard the bathroom door open once again. But before it closed she heard Stephie's voice. "If you decide you want to talk or need a shoulder, I'm here for you." Then the door closed and Becca resumed her sobbing quietly, just as she was doing as she lay there in her bed as she felt herself slip back into a light sleep.

Once again consciousness crept back in as Becca's mind faced yet another time when Stephie had come to her rescue.

It was the morning of the Spring Dance. All of Becca's friends had been shopping for weeks to find just the right dress. It was important that the "rite of passage" of graduating from middle school to high school was done in style. Becca's father had taken her to the mall to try to find her perfect dress for her as well. Becca had found what she considered to be the dress that would make her a part of the group she so desperately wanted to belong to.

She was amazed after trying it on as she looked in the full length mirror at herself. She almost couldn't recognize the reflection as it starred back at her. She stayed in the dressing room checking every detail of her appearance. The light yellow color of the bodice draped with a delicate lace seemed to shimmer in the dressing room lights as she turned from side to side. The shorter length of the skirt of the dresses gave her legs such definition when she stepped into the light yellow high heeled shoes. The clerk has suggested a wider belt to go with the dress than what was designed to go with it. She had resisted the idea but gave in on trying it out with the dress. Even upon adding the wider white belt, she was even more delighted in how it changed the shape of her body. She couldn't believe how beautiful the girl in the mirror was.

After starring at herself for quite awhile, Becca quickly opened her purse and grabbed her bundle of hair pins and piled her hair on the top of her head. The ends of her hair fell perfectly into place as she placed the curls where she wanted them. She took out her makeup and placed it on the dressing room chair and began to create a work of art. She released a long, deep breath and walked out of the dressing room to gain approval of her Dad.

Her Dad's eyes opened widely as she gazed at Becca with amazement. She knew in that moment that she was not only beautiful to herself, but to her Dad as well. A voice came from behind her, "Becca, you look absolutely wonderful". It was Stephie. Only a few short seconds later, Becca could tell by the change of her Dad's expression that there was a problem. "Becca, you are stunning in that dress, but after talking to the clerk, there isn't any way I can afford it right now since I got laid off from my job."

Becca nodded her head and proceeded to the dressing room filled with disappointment.

Several minutes later she rejoined her Dad as they headed through the store toward the front entrance. On her way out she heard the clerk reply to another customer, "M'am, this is everything the young lady left in the dressing room. Is there anything else you would like to purchase?"

Without turning around Becca's eyes filled with tears as she heard Stephie reply to the clerk, "No, that will be all."

Becca was devastated that Stephie was buying the dress, shoes, and belt for herself. Now she would never be able to buy it for *herself.*

Later that afternoon Becca's heard her door bell ring and moments later her Dad called her downstairs. Her Dad said someone was at the door for her. "I don't feel like seeing anyone right now", she replied to her Dad. "I know you have decided not to go to the dance tonight, but Becca, I really think you should go to the door", her Dad said insistently.

Becca reluctantly opened the door and was shocked to find the clerk from the store, who had insisted she try on the wider belt with the dress she couldn't get, standing there. The lady smiled and handed her two boxes wrapped with shiny paper. She gazed at the woman not able to speak. The visiting store clerk happily blurted out, "Another person shopping in our store earlier today noticed how wonderful you looked in this dress and shoes. They also noticed you left the store without purchasing these items. They thought so much of you they purchased these items themselves and asked me to deliver them to you. You have such a good friend. The young lady didn't buy anything for herself. She only had enough for one outfit. She was so happy; you would have thought she had found the perfect dress for herself. You rarely find friends like that."

Becca could feel the edges of her lips turning up as she drifted back into unconsciousness while summing up her final thoughts about Stephie. She had to admit to herself that Stephie had always had a kind hearted friend that looked out for her all those years ago. She was just too stubborn to admit it to herself until now. Taking a long, deep breath and groaning with loss as she faintly cried, "I'm sorry, Stephie. You *were* a friend to me. I didn't see it and was blinded by jealousy. I just didn't know how to be a friend to you. I couldn't even be a friend to myself. I would love for you to be here now. Even though I never told you, the concern you showed for me did help. I just wish I hadn't been so stubborn."

Becca fell into a deep sleep. But, it wouldn't last for long.

Chapter 3

Once again Becca was half asleep and half awake as she recalled these words coming out of her mouth over twenty years ago, "You may have given birth to me. But, you decided to leave when I was so small that I couldn't even remember you being her for me at all. Giving birth doesn't make you a parent. Why on earth, after all these years, would you even *start* to think that *I* would want you to be a part of my life now?"

Becca was less than three years old when her mother had decided that being a mother and a wife was not what she wanted to be. The only parent she had was her Dad. Her grandmother had done a wonderful job of filling in as a mother figure for her since her mother had left.

Becca knew exactly how she felt about this woman when she spoke those harsh words to her upon their first and only encounter since her mother had abandoned her *and* her father. Her mother had gotten in contact with her grandmother to find out where Becca lived. She couldn't believe that this woman she didn't even know had the guts to visit her out of the blue with—no warning.

Becca wanted nothing to do with her mother. And she had made sure this was very clear to the woman who was now trying to be a part of her life. But, this stranger was very persistent, as persistent as Becca was—if not more. She would not give up until Becca would acknowledge that she was indeed her mother.

Over the course of the next few years following this initial encounter, Becca has received numerous cards for various occasions, letters, cards and gifts from her mother. Each time Becca has returned them to the post office and requested they been returned to their sender.

After a few years the cards and letters had come to an end. Becca was relieved after a period of time that this bombardment had stopped. It had been her mother's decision to leave—for whatever reason she had. But, it would be her decision if or when her mother would be allowed back into her life. She had done without her mother all these years. She had no reason that she couldn't do without her now.

A couple of years after she had stopped receiving letters from her mother, Becca's grandmother came over for what she had called a serious talk. Becca's grandmother had brought a box with her to "just take a look at", as she grandmother had put it. Becca was speechless to find that her grandmother had brought the box full of cards and letters—the ones she had returned to her mother all those times. Her grandmother explained that Becca's mother asked her to keep them until Becca was a older and give them to her when she thought the time was right.

"Grams, I know you think you are doing what is best for me. But, I just don't have any interest in reading all this. I know this woman is your daughter, but I want nothing to do with her. If I did, I would have read them when they were sent to me the first time." Becca folded the top of the box and starting looking for tape to seal it once again.

"Becca, I had an idea you would feel this way, so I took the liberty of bringing one of the letters. Do an old lady a favor and just let me read this to you. It isn't just for your benefit, but for mine as well. Trust me. There is something that *I* have to confess to you and this is the best way I know how."

Being totally confused about what her grandmother needed to confess to, Becca silently nodded her head with approval. Her grandmother began to read;

Becca,

I have tried for so long to try to make up for leaving you when you were so young. I have written this letter in hopes that someday you will find it in your heart to give me a few moments to say what has been hidden inside *my* heart for so long.

You were so small and I was so young. You were my life. I loved you so much, but I guess I didn't love myself very much. I had made so many mistakes. I had hurt so many people that meant so much to me—your father included.

I won't go into details of the person I had become, but you have to believe this, I was so lost. I was blinded by so many things. I won't make any excuses for the choices I made back then. However, I will take responsibility and admit that I was so, so wrong.

The choices I made deprived you of a mother. And for that I am sincerely sorry. I was convinced that I was making the right decision by leaving. I was also convinced that I was doing what I did for *your* best interest.

You see, there was such a battle over whether or not you would live with me or your father. We were both so caught up in who would win custody of you. Every time I turned around your father would file papers and the sheriff would knock at my door. He would take you out of my arms to return you to your father. It was a vicious cycle, Becca. I had no choice but to in return file papers in desperation to get you back. This went on for months.

Each time this happened, I was devastated seeing the way you cried as you were pried out of my arms. I knew it was the same when you were taken from your father to be returned to me. I couldn't let this continue. We both loved you so much. Neither of us wanted to give you up for even a second.

I couldn't watch you go through this anymore. It was tearing me apart. I realized I wasn't putting you first in having you dragged back and forth. I was putting myself first.

After talking to the only person that I knew would listen without condemning me, I decided to sign custody of you over to your father. The only solution that I thought would work was do what was needed to keep things equal between your father and I. This was the hardest thing I had ever done and it is still the hardest thing I have done since.

I knew your father and your grandmother loved you so much. I knew I wouldn't ever have to worry about you having what you needed. I hope you can forgive me some day. I had to diminish from your life in order not to cause you continuous disruption and instability. I pray you will understand, I have and will always love you.

Always,
Mom

Gram's folded the letter, placed it back in the envelope as Becca sat and stared at her without saying a word. Her grandmother didn't look up to see her reaction. They both sat silently for what seemed to be hours.

Never had she imagined that this had been what had caused her mother to leave without being a part of her life even in the slightest way. No one had ever wanted to talk about it, even when she had questioned so many times over the years. She felt as if . . . well she didn't know what to feel. But, she finally had an answer and wouldn't have to come up with anymore reasons or questions regarding what had been kept a mystery for so long.

Amid the silence, with her head still hanging down, her grandmother began to speak.

"Becca, I have to ask you to forgive your mother for leaving you all those years ago. It is so important to me that you do so for this reason; I am the one she trusted to talk to before she made the decision to leave. She was in such much pain. We both saw you suffering being dragged back and forth. Neither of us could bare having you hurt. If you forgive your mother, then I will know you have forgiven me as well for my part in her leaving."

Dazed, she asked her grandmother, "What part did you have in her leaving?"

"I didn't know when we spoke that morning that she was thinking about leaving. She didn't tell me that thought had even crossed her mind. I had no way of knowing. I guess I should have somehow known", she replied with tears filling her eyes.

"I didn't know she would apply our conversation to the situation with you. There were three of us there that day—myself, and a lady in my Bible Study group, along with your mother.

The question was asked, "What should one do in a situation where pain is being caused to another?" I replied that if one had it within their control to bear the pain for the other, it would be the appropriate to do so. To sacrifice one's self for another would be the ultimate reflection of love, as Christ sacrificed himself for us."

Becca's grandmother continued, "I have held so much guilt since that day. I should have taken the time to talk to your mother after my company had left, but I was in such a hurry to start dinner for your grandfather. I have always regretted not taking the time to explain to her that she couldn't sacrifice herself to stop the evident pain she knew you were feeling, unless she could so do without causing you pain in another way. I really didn't stop to think I may have needed to do so. The conversation was about something all together different."

"Becca, this is what your mother had been trying to tell you since her first visit with you. But, you never gave her the chance. All the letters in the box say the same thing. The only one that is different is the one I just read to you. This is the one she mailed to me just after she left with a note for me to read it to you at the time she designated for it to be read. She truly believed she was doing the right thing. She believed she was taking your pain upon herself."

There was another long period of silence.

When Becca's grandmother finally looked up at Becca, she was astonished to see that it was as if a light bulb had come on for Becca. She was hoping that she could finally see that her mother had not left to hurt her. But rather to save her from further hurt, even if it was done so misguided.

Becca began to open the box and search the envelope fronts. There were so many different addresses from over the years of her mother sending her letters. In desperation she quickly looked at her grandmother with longing in her voice, "Tell me which one of these addresses is the current one. I have to know. Do you have her phone number? I have to speak to her!"

Crying once more, her grandmother answered, "It's too late, Becca. I'm sorry. It's too late.

Your mother gave me directions not to give you the letter I read out loud to you until she wrote me giving me permission to do so. I received a letter this morning from someone I didn't know, after not hearing from your mother for months. The woman who wrote, said it was your mother's request to give you the letter I was holding for you. She also requested also that I tell you that your mother passed away just a couple of days ago. She had struggled with cancer for quite awhile."

Becca, eyes grew dim—as if the light bulb had turned off once again. Her grandmother stayed until she was finished crying. When Becca was all alone once more, she sat down with the box of letters and slowly read through them all—soaking in every way her mother phrased parts of her speech. If she had been so stubborn in not wanting to know her mother, she would be even more stubborn to read and re-read the letters trying to learn the smallest detail about her she could find in these pages in an attempt to know anything about her that she could.

Becca, once again sobbed quietly as she yearned for the time back, she had been offered to get to know her mother, which she had thrown away.

Chapter 4

Becca was now wide awake as she lifted herself to a sitting position. She realized that all the people who had really loved her, she had pushed away. It had seemed right for her to do so at the time. She always had what seemed to be good reasons. But, she found herself questioning herself as to how she had come to some of the conclusions she had in so many instances in her life. She was asking herself what things had she neglected to include in her decision making process in the past.

Becca pulled to the surface memories and words that had been etched in her mind from the only mother figure in her life as she was growing up, her grandmother.

Becca's grandmother was the one who sat on her bedside when she had been sick throughout the years of her childhood and teenage years. She had been there to take her back and forth to school. She spent weekends with her learning how to cook and do housework whenever her father had to go out of town on business trips. Although her grandmother was small in statute and very petite, it seemed to Becca that she was the strongest and most reliable person in her world.

Throughout some many difficult times in her life, her grandmother had tried her best to guide her with relationships, friendships, personal decisions and financial decisions. At this point, she couldn't figure out for the life of her why she hadn't listened to her grandmother's advise and direction. She had just assumed that her grandmother was so much older, that whatever process she had used to guide her own life had to be outdated and out of touch with the reality of the world as it was during these crucial times for Becca.

Becca thought back to the times she had helped her grandmother in the kitchen fixing homemade chocolate pies, banana puddings, fresh loaves of bread, pepperoni rolls with sour dough bread, and toll house cookies.

Becca remembered the evenings when she had gotten hungry and her grandmother refused to let her have cookies or sweets because she had already eaten some of them after dinner. Instead her grandmother would pull out the largest cast iron frying pan, place it on the stove and heat the oil. Then she would peel a few potatoes and slice them into thin, round sections and fry them to perfection.

Becca missed the talks and how her grandmother would go out of her way to spend time with her even when she had so many other things to do. She longed to have that closeness with someone again and feel safe and secure.

"Maybe I was wrong", Becca said as she slid back down in the bed, curling up on her side and hugging the pillow. "After all Grams always did seem to have her life much more together than I do. She always seemed happy and had a peace about her, no matter the situation."

Becca felt herself slowly drifting in and out of sleep and words her grandmother had said to her over the years.

As she lay there, Becca remembered being mad at her father. She didn't recall her exact age, but she knew she was very young. She tried to remember the exact reason why she had been so mad, but she couldn't. One thing she did remember was the look of hurt and disappointment she saw on her father's face as she spoke these words to him.

"I don't like living here. I am not happy now and have never been happy here. I don't love you!" Becca was staring at her Dad as if she expected him to give in to her and give her whatever it had been she thought she deserved. Instead her Dad had simply shook his head while taking a deep breath. He slowly closed his eyes and she thought she saw the smallest of tears squeeze through a tiny opening as he began to open them once again. He opened his mouth to speak.

Becca was certain that he was going to let her have it—not what she wanted, but definitely what she deserved. Instead, he took another long breath and upon releasing it, he turned and walked out of the room.

Becca remembered feeling so alone. But worse than that she remembered feeling disappointed in herself. This was the first time her Dad had ever looked disappointed in her. She didn't like the feeling of being so alone. But, somehow at such a young age, she knew she had decided to push that feeling away so she would never have to deal with it again. So, once again, she returned to anger in order to mask this new feeling she had.

Several days had gone by, and still her Dad hadn't said much to her. Thinking back on it, she realized he probably didn't know how to handle her temper tantrums. She had tried the same strategy with him as he was trying with him. She only talked when spoken to. She tried her best to beat him at his own game. She remember wanting to jump into his arms and tell him how sorry she was so he would return to smiling every time she walked into the room.

About two weeks later, her Dad had to go out of town on a business trip. He arranged again for her grandmother to keep her while he was gone. Every time he dropped her off at her grandmother's house, deep inside she feared that he would never return home. The thought of never seeing him again was very scary for her.

When he dropped her off at her grandmother's for this particular trip. He reminded her to behave and listen to her grandmother. It hurt her when her Dad said to her in a very stern voice, "Becca, no temper tantrums while I am gone. Respect your grandmother. Do you hear me?"

Although she still wanted nothing more than to jump into his arms and ask him to remember to bring her something back from his trip, she only replied in a monotone voice, "I hear you."

Becca loved spending time at her grandmother's house. But this time, because of the argument with her father, she wasn't looking forward to it like she had in the past. This time she longed for her father to stay home. Her fear of him not returning was stronger than it had ever been.

Grams would always take her on their special outings. This time was no different. As soon as her Dad had left Gram's announced, "Time to sneak out of here for awhile. Are you with me Becca?"

Grams had lived just on the edge of town. And since the town wasn't very big they could walk everywhere they went on their outings. Grams always called the time she stayed with her while her father was away "Opportunity Time."

This Opportunity Time started about the same as all the others before. Grams telling her to hurry up and finish her breakfast so they could head to town. Just as every other outing, first they would walk past the church. Grams would tell her how much she loved the way the pastor preached. She always carried on and on about how the church was her second home.

Grams did spend a lot of time at the church. There was always a social or special event going on. Grams did so many things there. If Grams wasn't at home, chances were she was at the church—unless, of course, she was out on an outing with Becca.

Next they would walk past the Feed Store. Grams would always hold her hand as she climbed on top of the retaining wall and balanced herself the whole length of it. Grams never neglected to ask her if she wanted to go inside and help her down from the wall when nearing the entrance of the parking lot. She would always answer, "Sure do, Grams. I want to see how many rabbits they have this time. Maybe Dad will get *me* a rabbit when I'm a little bit older."

As they walked past the rabbit cages, she would always pick out her favorite one and dream of one day having one of her own. Oh, how she wanted a black and white rabbit. They were the cutest of all.

Grams would remind her of how each one of the rabbits belonged to God. And, that He had made each one just a little different than the next. Most of the time, she would question the difference between the white rabbits. To her, the white ones all looked the same. But, Gram's would assure her that even though they all looked the same, there was something different, but in one way they were the same—they were created by God just as everything in the world was.

Next Grams would take her to the salon to get her hair trimmed. This part of their outings she wasn't that fond of. She wanted her hair to grow long. But, Grams would always insist that every time she got her hair trimmed, especially her bangs, her eyes seemed bigger and were more beautiful than they had before she got them trimmed.

She couldn't argue with that since she loved her grandmother doting over her.

It never failed that Grams would announce as they neared the diner near the middle of town how famished she was. She always wondered if Grams could eat an entire bear as she claimed she could. Each time this thought came into her mind, she just giggle out loud. Grams would always ask her what was so funny. She never told Grams what she was thinking and just replied, "Nothing Grams."

After lunch, Grams would always ask her if she wanted to catch the matinee at the movie.

They would walk by the marquis to see what was playing. The times they did find a movie they wanted to see, Grams would order popcorn loaded with butter, and two large cherry Icees.

Gram's half of the popcorn was always gone before the movie even started. That made Becca wonder even more if Grams could really eat a bear.

Becca remembered Grams commenting on a road sign on their way home that particular day as they stopped at a corner to cross the street on their way back to Grams house.

"Becca, how many people do you think stop to think about this sign?"

"I don't know, Grams?" Becca replied. "Yield", said Grams. "If others thought about this sign the way I do, they would sure get along better." Grams said smiling and nodding her head.

"What does a traffic sign have to do with life—other than driving", Becca asked her grandmother.

"Oh, it has everything to do with life, Becca."

"Such as . . . ?" Becca questioned her grandmother as to challenge her to prove her point.

"Yield is exactly what God has told us to do. There are a couple of ways I see God in that sign reminding us to listen to him. First He tells us to yield our life to Him—to His direction. Just as the sign is to remind drivers to yield to other cars to let other cars go first, this is what God wants us to do. He wants us to yield and let Him lead the way and wants us to follow." Grams explained to Becca with her eyes lit up with excitement. Becca still challenging her Grams further asked, "What else Grams?"

"Well Becca, the way I see it, this sign was put here to warn driver's of danger. Other cars come flying by and if a car pulls out without thinking and doesn't have this sign to remind them to pay attention before pulling out into traffic, then they just may get hurt very badly. We sometimes don't see danger coming because it is just out of our sight. By the time we see it there is a greater possibility of harm. That's what happens if you rely on your own understanding in a situation, Becca. People tend to ignore or forget without having some extra help, even in situations they have been in before. Most people make decisions based upon what they can see.

They don't even consider there are things they are unaware of that can impact that decision. But, if we yield to God, and follow His direction, we can be assured that because He knows all things and sees all things, we will be safer. He loves us so much that He wants to keep us from harm, Becca. But the only way he can keep us from harm is if we yield to His direction first."

Grams and Becca had returned home. They sat in the rockers as the sun began to go down. Grams had just told Becca it was about time to get washed up so she would be nice and clean. Becca remembered not wanting to follow her grandmother's direction about washing up and grumbled. Grams reminded her of the yield sign earlier in the day.

"Becca, I don't want to argue with you about listening to me. However, I want you to understand that you have to learn to follow direction with simple things, such as washing up when you're told to do so. I am only teaching you to follow directions. God had commanded that we are to teach you these things when you are young to prepare you to follow directions later in life. It is to prepare you to listen and to yield to His direction. That way when you are old enough to yield your life to Him, you will be able to better follow His directions so he can keep you safer."

Becca could find no way to argue with her grandmother's words. Just as Becca started to open the screen door to go inside and be obedient to her grandmother, Grams spoke up, "I know you are upset with your father right now and you are giving Him the silent treatment." Becca replied with a slight bit of defiance, "He is not talking to me much either, Grams. I don't think it is very fair."

Grams motioned for her to return to her chair. Upon doing so, Grams spoke, "Becca, parents react much in the same way God does to His children. God provides all things. Without him there would be nothing. We would have nothing. He gave us life. He expects us to respect and love Him just for the simple fact He is God and He is the Creator, regardless of whether or not he chooses to give us the things we want. Sometimes He holds back on giving us the things we want. It could be as simple as He knows that we are not ready for what we ask for or that we cannot handle the unseen dangers of getting what we want. When we get angry at Him for withholding something from us, we cause a distance between us and God because of our own disobedience.

The distance is not caused because God did anything wrong, but because we have done wrong by not appreciating all He has done for us."

"Now, go wash up and take some time to think about what I told you. See if you can begin to understand."

As Becca drifted into a deeper sleep, she could remember her grandmother speaking about God in the manner she had that day. There was so much authority in her voice. There was so much certainty. She knew even back then that her grandmother somehow *knew* her words were truth. But, she didn't know how.

Chapter 5

Becca rolled over in her bed finding herself awake once more. It was as if this night would last forever and she would never finish reliving her past. In the darkness she whispered hopefully, "Alright, one more time, I guess. Then maybe I can get some interrupted sleep."

Becca was going to camp. Her grandmother and father somehow got the money together and was able to afford to let her go with her new friend to teen camp. She wasn't sure if she would enjoy the week or not, but was taken in by Nicole's description of the camp. She really did like Nicole. Somehow she seemed so much different than her other friends. She was excited to be going away for a whole week. This was the first time she would be away from home without her Dad or grandmother. She was almost eighteen years old and it was about time she saw or did something *kind of* on her own.

Nicole had made the camp sound so wonderful. There was a lake where they would be allowed to swim everyday and play water games. Nicole had told her they had a swing, that would swing out over the lake, which held several people at a time. There were obstacle courses and uphill climbs where the hills were packed with mud. The food was wonderful according to Nicole. She was looking forward to doing paint ball wars, going on the hikes and sitting by a camp fire. Most of all she was looking forward to sharing a cabin and goofing off with Nicole for a whole week.

The only thing she wasn't so sure about was the chapel times. Nicole had told her that the day always started off with breakfast and then it was off to chapel, then the day ended with chapel again.

Nicole described it as her favorite part of the camp. She loved the singing, the music, the fellowship and the skits. But, most of all she loved the preaching. She said it recharged her and enabled her to face life as they know it when she returned home.

Becca was afraid of the chapel part of the day. The only time she had ever gone to church was with her grandmother. She liked going but not for the same reason her grandmother did. She d*id not* go for the preaching. She liked going to see her friends and to be able to go to the teen activities. All of the teens in the group in her grandmother's church always took notes during the sermons. Becca had her sermon notebook as well, every Sunday she went. While the rest of the teens were writing down that the pastor had said, she would be writing a story of her own. Here and there she would write down a scripture reference whenever she would hear the pastor say in a loud voice, "Teens, look up at me. Make sure you write this down." She had asked one of her friends to nudge her when he did this so she wouldn't feel embarrassed if he decided to call her name out if she didn't look. This had been this case a couple of times in the past and she definitely didn't want it to happen again.

She was afraid of feeling like an idiot during at camp. Nicole had told her that there was a lot of small group meetings that took place over the course of the week. She guessed it was a good idea for those of them that wanted to discuss the Bible. She had decided she would keep quite unless she was absolutely sure in what she was saying.

After arriving, she felt out of place and a little left behind the whole day. She had none of the clothes or jewelry everyone else had. As the group made their way to their cabin after arriving at camp, she lagged behind everyone else in the group. Nicole had called out to her to join in on a group discussion while they were walking. She called back, "I'll be there in a few. I'm having trouble managing all of these bags. I'll figure it out in a minute though. Go ahead. I will catch up", as she smiled and waved Nicole ahead. She couldn't' help thinking she had made the wrong decision in coming to camp.

Once Becca got her bags where she could manage them, she paused to look at the surroundings. She had lived her whole life east of Raleigh where the landscape was flat. She was amazed by the mountain scenery. It was breathtaking.

The early morning air had a chill, even in the middle of the summer. The mountains in the distance were so alive with trees. The birds were singing loudly. It seemed as though there were hundreds of them singing at the same time creating a symphony of sound.

Becca could hear the babbling of a stream as the water flowed gently over the giant rocks.

It was so peaceful there.

Becca stopped for a minute just to take it all in. While she wasn't looking, one on the group counselors had came up beside her and tapped her on the shoulder. "This, Becca, is one of the reasons I love working here at the camp so much. God painted us a masterpiece to enjoy." The both paused for a moment to take one last look at the beauty of it all before they continued on their way toward the cabins which were a mile up the mountain.

The cabins were long and narrow inside. Two set of bunk beds lined the wall on each side.

At the back of the cabin was one bathroom with on small shower, on sink and mirror, and one toilet for eight teenage girls to share. Becca noticed a sign just beside the shower that read, "Shower Limit: Five minutes per camper". The front wall of the cabin was lined with lockers to store their things in.

While the other girls were talking and giggling, Becca slid past them in order to grab a top bunk.

The first day of camp was nothing like she had ever seen before. She had never seen a group of teenagers so fired up about God. The energy level they had made her exhausted just watching them. The thought to herself, "Most of these teens look like a walking billboard for Christ. Their t-shirts only have Bible verses on them. Even their bracelets reflected their attitude for God. I thought the older people where I live went so overboard with religion, but they aren't anything compared to this."

Nicole had been right, breakfast was wonderful. She hadn't seen so much food at a breakfast table in her entire life. Everyone filled their plates with bacon, sausage, eggs, pancakes, fruits and juice or milk. As they sat down, she had not been accustomed to saying grace before beginning to eat. She quickly filled her fork with eggs. Just before she got them to her mouth, the counselor for their table walked by and lightly touched her shoulder. She was very polite when she bent down to whisper, "We will say grace in just a second." None the less, she still felt a little embarrassed as Nicole leaned over and said, "Don't sweat it. Everyone is so hungry after the drive to get here. None of us really want to wait. We are starved." She lowered her fork and returned it beside the plate.

As soon as breakfast was over, everyone dashed quickly to empty their trays and headed to the chapel. There was electricity in the air as she entered the room. A sea of teens were raising their hands above their heads while swaying them and singing to Christian music she had never heard before. This music was more like the music she listened to but the message of the songs was definitely different. She liked it, but it was hard for her to join in on what seemed to be a festivity since she didn't know the music or the lyrics. She silently hoped to learn the music before the end of the week. But, most of all she hoped to find the happiness and joy she saw in others all around her.

The singing and swaying lasted for several minutes before the pastor stepped up onto the stage. After he was done with welcoming the church groups and going over some of the rules of the camp, he reminded them that this was a week to learn. He wanted them to really put some thought into what they heard during chapel—real thought, not just a fleeting moment of thought, but to roll what they learned over and over in their minds. He stressed how important this was to him. He had told them he wanted them to have real discussions that would lead to growth in their Christian walk during counseling sessions.

Although she couldn't recall his name, she did however, very vividly remember the first sermon of the week he preached. He had called his sermon "What is a *real* Christian?" His first question was, "What does a *real* Christian look like?" He proceeded with other questions which she vividly remembered as well. "How does a *real* Christian conduct their everyday life?" and ended with the question, "Can someone who doesn't know you tell that you are a real Christian?"

Becca had picked up her sermon note pad. This time she didn't write stories that she came up with on her own. She began to write what the pastor was saying. She was writing questions that came into her mind that she wanted answered in the columns of the pages.

She was sure the pastor would describe a real Christian looking and acting as all the other teens at camp looked and acted. She wanted to fit in, so she wanted to get it all written down so if she forgot she could go back and look.

The pastor started by saying how nice everyone looked in their Christian t-shirts and their *WWJD* bracelets and fish necklaces. He applauded how long it must have taken them to have chosen just the right shirt that said just the right thing. He also mentioned he was impressed to see that the clothing he had seen so far had been modest on the girls. He mentioned that he was glad to see that most everyone knew the lyrics of the music as they entered the chapel that morning. He praised the teens he had seen helping others carry their bags to their cabin. He over praised the teens who had lead their own group of teens in prayer just a few minutes earlier while at breakfast.

At that point Becca remembered sinking down into her seat. She thought to herself, "There's no way any of this describes me. Now I definitely know everyone can look at me and tell I have *no clue* what is going on here." She was beginning to feel really uncomfortable. She laid her sermon notebook down by her side after closing it feeling very dishearten.

Just before her thoughts slipped away to another place, the pastor shouted loudly, **"Can anyone tell me if there is a real Christian here? How can I tell?"** Becca thought to herself, "Is this guy mad. He just stood there and praised the appearance and actions of all these other teens."

The next second he announced, "I see all the things on all of you that would make someone assume you are a real Christian. But, can I see that you are the real deal when you don't have all this stuff on?"

Once again the pastor had her attention. She listened as he proceeded. Once again she picked up her notepad with pen in hand. She wrote in her notes the things she considered to be important:

> <u>What being a real Christian is **NOT**</u>
> Wearing Christian t-shirts
> Wearing Christian jewelry
> Praying out loud to impress others
> Helping others only when someone is watching

Showing compassion when it is convenient
Being charitable only when it profits you
Going to church on Sunday and talking the talk
Acting the way you want the rest of the week
Grumbling when being asked to do something
Being disobedient to you parents
Being disobedient to those who have authority over you
(Unless it goes against God's Word)
Using religion for self gain

<u>What being a real Christian **IS**</u>
Loving your enemies and praying for them
Giving even when you have little to give
Helping others because it comes from the heart
Reading God's Word daily
Meditating on God's Word constantly
Striving to grow spiritually
Praying earnestly
Yielding to His Will for your life
(If you are doing all these things then it is perfectly acceptable to have the t-shirts and jewelry. If you are not doing all these things then all the symbols worn for display is done in vain.)

Becca was beginning to like what she was hearing. The pastor had put things into a language she could understand. She knew he really wanted to get through to them on a level that they could understand. She was going to like it here at camp after all.

At the end of the service the pastor gave an alter call. She felt something she had never felt before. She was almost shaking. She checked her hands as they held the chair in front of her to make sure no one would notice the shaking sensation she had. She was good, if she couldn't see it then no one else could either. Then she noticed the palms of her hands were as if she had just taken them out of a bowl of water. She felt as if she was being pulled by something to go to the altar, but she was afraid. She stood her ground and did not budge. She knew she wanted to learn more. She found herself looking forward to the evening chapel.

The rest of the day was filled with activities. She couldn't believe how non-stop the day had been. There had been group games, softball, swimming, lunch, and more group activities.

She was exhausted by the time the loud speaker announced, "Fifteen minutes clean up time before dinner is served."

Becca noticed how stiff the calves of her legs were. She had been walking up and down the steep hills all day long. She wondered if she would be physically able to keep up for the rest of the week. But, as she thought about the sermon earlier that day, she resolved to make sure she would be able to attend all the chapel meetings—even if she had to miss out on the fun in between.

Following dinner, it was off to group session. She had been nervous beforehand at the thought of talking about something she knew little about to strangers. She was relieved that during the session, no one had probed her about what she knew concerning the Bible. She instead was able to listen to the other teens as they posed their questions to the group leaders. She listened to the devotional for the evening making sure not to miss a word. She reached down under her chair to grab her note pad only to realize she had left it and her Bible in the cabin.

"How can I ever remember the verses they want us to look up for next session without my note pad?" she remembered thinking. She was relieved when one of the counselors gave handouts to the entire group with the scripture list included on them.

The next forty-five minutes following group session was allotted for down time. It was explained during group session that this time should be used to review notes that had been taken at morning chapel and to look up scripture from group session to prepare themselves for chapel the next morning.

Becca was ready for chapel. She had memorized the list the pastor had given that morning. She looked up the verses on the handout and quickly made her notes. She decided to rest her legs by taking a short nap before the long walk back up the steep hill to chapel. She made Nicole promise to wake her up in plenty of time to make chapel. All she needed was a short nap.

She walked into the chapel wondering and eager for the next sermon. She was ready to learn. She felt as if she could not get enough of what the pastor had earlier in chapel. The pastor took his place.

But, instead of delivering an evening sermon as Becca had hoped, he introduced several camp counselors and asked them to take over. She felt disappointment as the group on stage began to lead them in song.

The counselors then asked for volunteers to help out with skits they were going to perform. Becca thought this to be silly in the beginning, but after sitting through the remainder of the program she had been given much more to think about. She was amazed that even though the skits had been funny, they were real life situations—situations she had found herself in before.

Once again her interest returned.

Chapter 6

Becca smiled to herself as she remembered enjoying the activities of her week at camp.

She chuckled to herself when thinking how dearly she loved the rest of the morning services. She thought to herself, "I learned so much. I had found something that I believed in. I was so on fire and ready to take on each new day not knowing what that day would hold. I believed in miracles and *expected* them to happen."

As each day of camp passed, she was less and less afraid to speak about Christ in front of the other teens and counselors. This had been the first time that she ever felt that she was not all alone.

Suddenly, Becca jumped up and turned on the lamp on the nightstand. She knew she had kept the sermon note pad from camp. She opened the closet door and pulled out the one box that she had packed up such a long time ago but never unpacked it again for some reason. Every time she cleaned things out, she just couldn't bring herself to throw it out with the other things.

After pulling the tape off the top, she reached down and found a red ribbon with a medallion. She rubbed her fingers across the words written on it and remembered how proud she had been when she received it. She read it aloud, "Most Christ Like". She wondered how she could have wandered so far away from something that had brought her so much happiness. It had been a short lived experience but it had meant the world to her when she was a teenager. The ribbon had faded from the bright vibrant red she remembered and it seemed tattered and torn—much like she felt.

She placed the ribbon around her neck as tears filled her eyes. She took a picture of Nicole and herself which had been taken the evening she had surrendered her life to Christ. Both her and Nicole were smiling from ear to ear but their faces were red and eyes swollen from crying as a result of her decision on that night—the most important decision of her life. She couldn't help thinking how full of life expectation she was for the future as she looked in the picture. That too had faded, just like the ribbon.

The final article she pulled out of the long forgotten box was her sermon notebook. She carried it with her back to bed and opened the book, but not before placing the picture she had found against the lamp on her nightstand.

She fluffed her pillows to be just right before beginning to read the sermon notes. She carefully reviewed the page titled, "*Sermon One*" and remembered how it drew her in. She ran her fingers over the words as she read them. She sighed before turning the next page.

"*Sermon Two*", she whispered. She ran her fingers over the questions and outline of the second morning of camp sermons. She drifted back in time once more. All the feelings she had at that time flooded her whole being, even now as she began to read the words written so long ago;

> *Question 1—How do you know if you are a Christian?*
> *Question 2—How do you know you are going to heaven?*
> *Question 3—What are you trusting in to get you to heaven?*
> *Question 4—What steps did you take in achieving Salvation?*
> *(Notice the word you is underlined in all the above questions.)*

She remember the camp pastor saying, "There is nothing *you* have done or can do in the future to ensure you are going to heaven except one thing—making the most important decision of your life. Making this decision is **your** defining moment of who and what you are. Failure to make this decision, is by default, making a decision in itself. Now let me begin to explain."

"I am going to answer all the questions at one time. If you have never followed along with a sermon before today and taken notes, I suggest this is the morning. If they don't have an impact on you today, I will pray that they will soon."

Becca returned her attention to the words she had taken down and continued to read the points as she wrote them that morning;

Pastor Comments

- Salvation is a free gift. It is not earned. No amount of charity or good works ensures it.
- The free gift comes from God. The gift is received through Christ. The only part you have in salvation is nothing more than choosing to accept the gift.
- There is no other way to salvation except the blood of Christ.
- Christ shed his blood and took your iniquities (sin) upon himself on the cross.
- You must acknowledge that you are a sinner
- You must ask God for forgiveness of your sins and repent with a pure heart
- You must believe that Christ is the Son of God, was crucified, and rose again the third day.
- God longs for all to be saved.

Scripture References

- John 3:16—"For God so loved the world that He gave His only begotten Son. Whosoever believeth in Him should not perish, but have everlasting life."
- John 14:6—"I am the way, the truth and the life, no man cometh to the Father but by me.
- Romans 3:23—"For all have sinned, and come short of the glory of God"
- Ecclesiastes 7:20—"For there is not a just man upon the earth, that doeth good, and sinneth not."
- Romans 6:23—"For the wages of sin is death, but the gift of God is eternal life through Jesus Christ our Lord"

- Romans 5:8-10—"But God commended his love toward us; in that, while were were yet sinners, Christ died for us. Much more then, being now justified by his blood, we shall be saved from the wrath through him. For if, when we were enemies, we were reconciled to God by the death of his Son, much more, being reconciled, we shall be saved by his life.'
- Revelation 3:20—"Behold, I stand at the door, and knock: if any man hear my voice, and open the door, I will come in to him, and will sup with him, and he with me."
- Romans 10:9-13—"That if thou shalt confess with thy mouth the Lord Jesus, and shalt believe in thine heart that God raised him from the dead, thou shalt be saved. For with the mouth confession is made unto salvation. For the scripture saith, Whosoever believeth on him shall not be ashamed. For there is no difference between the Jew and the Greek; for the same Lord over all is rich unto all that call upon him. For whosoever shall call upon the name of the Lord shall be saved."

Assurance Scripture

1 John 5:13—"These things I have written unto you that believe on the name of the Son of God; that *ye may know* that ye have eternal life, and that ye may believe on the name of the Son of God."

Her heart was burdened. She knew she had pushed away what she had learned so many years ago. She turned the lamp off as she was falling into a light sleep, she went over and over these words in her mind before drifting once again into sleep. Her final thought before drifting off was, "Even though the pages in the notebook have turned yellow and the ink has faded, the words written within, from all those years ago are still alive and have not changed."

Chapter 7

Becca awaken from what seemed to be another long sleep. She glanced at her clock only to find that she had only dozed off for a few minutes, just as before. She returned to the note pad.

She flipped through the pages before laying the book to the side. Anger at herself filled her being for letting go of what was once so precious. She couldn't understand why she had gotten so far away from the place she had been during camp that year.

Her mind drifted to only a year later. That year was filled with disappointments for her and personal struggles. She had lost her best friend. Nicole had gone to college after deciding to give her life to God totally to become a missionary. She had moved to a country which had to be kept confidential until she returned home to report on how her travels and mission had went.

In the meantime, Becca had hopes of finding a better job than what she had in the small town where she lived. Shortly thereafter she moved to the city to fulfill her dreams. She never heard from Nicole again.

Following her move to the city and several weeks of searching for an office position, she realized that everyone that came from a small town must have had the same idea she had. The competition for office jobs was fierce.

Yet after finding a different job than office work, she was still happy that she had found a job, even if it hadn't been what she had hoped for. Waiting tables would have to do until something better came along.

After working at waiting tables at a diner for several months, she found something she enjoyed much more—working, private duty, sitting with elderly patients. The pay was much better and the was a welcome change from satisfying hundreds of people a day to satisfying just one.

She liked working with elderly patients. They seemed to appreciate everything that she did for them. She often times wished she had gone to college to get a degree, but rather decided that she just wanted to bring, what she considered to be more meaningful, individual attention into how she could help. Although the turnover rate in these positions were high, she thought it would better serve the patients she would work for by just being a friend and by filling in for a family member who was too busy to be with them as much as they wanted. That is how she met Mrs. Cauldron.

For the most part, she was happy working for and attending to Mrs. Cauldron over the next several months. She would start each morning by fixing breakfast. Oatmeal and toast was the favorite every morning for her patient. While Becca cleaned up the kitchen, Mrs. Cauldron would talk about her husband and the things they had done before he had passed away. Mrs. Cauldron had dementia and had trouble remembering details of the current day, but her memory of the past was extraordinarily vivid.

Sometimes Mrs. Cauldron's stories were memories of parties for special occasions they had attended or of trips they had taken in their younger years. She often wondered if Mrs. Cauldron knew that she had a unique way of getting a point across to her about something. She could use a totally different situation that applied somewhere else in her own life.

She remember a story about Mr. and Mrs. Cauldron having a barbecue for several friends when their daughter was turning twenty. Her daughter had brought a "young man", as Mrs. Cauldron had put it, with her to the party. Somehow the conversation turned to God and salvation during the party which lead to Mr. Cauldron questioning the young man whether or not he was saved. The young man had insisted he was. But upon answering Mr. Cauldron's question of whether or not he was doing anything for God or was he letting God do everything to him, the young man wasn't sure what to say. He only replied that he wasn't sure what he should do, or what he could do.

Becca had asked at that point, "What did your husband tell him, Mrs. Cauldron?" She was curious what the answer had been herself. Mrs. Cauldron sat up to attention and said with a strong, loud voice in an attempt to imitate her husband, "Well, son. If you are in a sea of rough waters and the waves are crashing down upon you in every direction as if to utterly destroy you and you call out to God to save you; then a boat appears out of nowhere and you climb inside to safety, what do you do? Do you just sit there in the boat going nowhere because you are out of the waves and are safe? NO, you don't just sit there in the boat doing nothing!"

Somehow Mrs. Cauldron could tell that Becca didn't understand. She looked at Becca and said, "Come here young lady and I will explain." Becca walked over to her and leaned her head down to hear Mrs. Cauldron whisper, "The boat is a picture of salvation."

Becca questioned Mrs. Cauldron as to what would one do after they find safety in salvation. She thought at the time she would never forget the answer she was given. "Becca, God offers salvation during our storms. Our storm is life. He is always offering us salvation. Some will choose His safety and some will not. When you choose to follow Him, He is deserving of your faithfulness and respect. He expects you to love Him as He loves you. He sacrificed Himself by dying on the cross to give you new life. It is appointed for man to die only once. The Bible says when you choose Him, you are made brand new. The former you passes away and you are a new creature."

Mrs. Cauldron continued, "He wants us to cast the cares of this world on Him and forsake the things that we want and pursue the things of God. By this I mean, to enrich the Kingdom of God. He tells us we are to do this by telling others about Him and His sacrifice for our sakes. I guess you could finish my husband's story by saying, you should take the boat and search for others who are drowning, too."

Becca lay there, staring at a small beam of light coming from beneath her blind. She thought to herself how dim the light was. It was barely noticeable. She thought that it would go overlooked and un-noticed unless you were looking for it. "What if", she thought, "you have to be in the darkest of times to be able to see the light?" This question brought back to her memory a conversation she had with Mrs. Cauldron during a weekend stay after Mrs. Cauldron had had surgery and her daughter was away.

It was a cool summer evening—just about dusk. She had made lemonade for herself and Mrs. Cauldron. She had wheeled Mrs. Cauldron onto the small upper deck and covered her legs with a beach towel to block the coolness from her while watching the sun go down that evening.

From the deck there was a beautiful view of the lake. You could see all the boats after they came in for the day. The owners and their families seemed relaxed as they docked and gathered their things for their drives home.

Becca had gotten tickled at a young girl who had gotten sunburned on their day of boating. The girl kept dropping her belongings as she walked up the dock. She was straggling behind her parents as the sun hovered just above the water in the background. Becca had pointed her out to Mrs. Cauldron as the girl once again tugged at the bottom of her swim suit to keep it from touching the sunburn. Every time the girl tugged at her suit, she would drop several things from her arms, bend over to pick them up, take a few steps then tug again repeating the same process. The two of them were laughing as she told Mrs. Cauldron that even the sea gulls flying over head seemed to be just as tickled as they were at the sight of the girl.

As the sun went down behind the water, Mrs. Cauldron commented that the solar light on the lower deck no longer gave off much light. She offered to go and check the light but Mrs. Cauldron insisted that it was fine. Mrs. Cauldron had asked her to refill her lemonade as it had just begun to get dark. While she was inside, the phone rang. It was Mrs. Cauldron's daughter.

She was excited that Becca had gotten her mother to go out onto the deck.

She walked back onto the deck and asked Mrs. Cauldron if it was getting too cool for her.

She replied that she wanted to wait just a little while longer before going in. She had told her that there was something that she wanted her to see. After awhile, she reminded Mrs. Cauldron that she really shouldn't sit outside for too long. She insisted still on another few minutes and then she assured her that as soon as she was able to point something out to her she would retire for the evening.

It was finally time for the mystery to be unveiled to her. "What had they sat there so long for?" she thought as Mrs. Cauldron spoke up. "Becca, look at that old solar light of mine. Do you remember how dim it was just a little while ago? You know, it is so funny to me that it seems as though just when I think it is about to flicker out and is of no more good, something happens to it. Just look at it. There is plenty of light to see by now."

She had asked, as if playing along, "What do you mean Mrs. Cauldron? Is there a point you are trying to make?" Mrs. Cauldron's voice turned serious as she addressed her this time, "Becca, you told me once that you believe in God and you had prayed for His salvation." Becca nodded her head in response. "You also told me that you weren't so sure God would be able to use you for anything because you quit reading your Bible and going to church." She again nodded. With a stern voice Mrs. Cauldron continued, "Dear, that light was dim and looked to be of no use to anyone earlier this evening. But, now it is shinning as bright as any other light out here in the dark. I know you've told me you have had a lot of turmoil in your life. But, let me explain something to you, child. You can put a light in a dark room and it will drive the darkness away from it. What many don't realize when it comes to their own dark times is; when a light is lit, even if it has dimmed to just a flicker of its former self, no matter how much darkness is poured onto it, that darkness can't drive the light away. In fact, the more darkness that is poured onto the flickering light, the brighter that light gets." Mrs. Cauldron nodded her head quickly and then asked her to take her in so she could retire for the evening.

Becca laughed out loud, in the dark, still lying in her bed staring at the flicker of light streaming in from underneath her blind.

Chapter 8

Becca's mind was racing now. She was going back and forth in time. She had stopped trying to hold back the memories. She had begun to embrace them. They no longer tormented her. They reminded her of a time in her life where she was compassionate, caring, loving, and kind. She lay in anticipation as she waited to drift off to sleep again and awaking to relive another chapter of her life. Yet deep inside her soul, something was still missing. Something was grabbing at her. She felt as if she were wrestling with something that needed to come out—something that had been waiting a long time. Something she kept buried out of fear.

"ICE CREAM!" Becca heard these words in her mind. Her Grandfather shouted, "ICE CREAM!" She heartily laughed out loud as she remembered the whole conversation with her Grandfather when she was in her early twenties.

She had gone home to attend her cousin Bobby's wedding just shortly after moving from home. After the festivities of the ceremony she announced to her grandparents that she had met someone in the city. She told them how handsome he was and all about his job at the hospital.

She was trying to go into grave detail her new man's life when her grandfather stopped her in her tracks and bluntly asked, "Bec, what church does this boy go to?" She answered by saying that if she recalled correctly he didn't go to church anymore. But remarked the most important thing is that he believed in God. She explained that he had been saved earlier that year, but with work and college, he didn't have time to attend church anymore. After her grandfather's reaction, she was too embarrassed to tell her grandparents that she had been rather busy as well and had been neglecting attending Sunday service at the moment.

Her grandfather had frowned at her after explaining her new boyfriend's reasoning for not going to church. "Gramps, he's got the basics right doesn't he? He is saved. That's what matters, right?" she said trying to lighten his mood. "That's where you're wrong, Bec. He's only got the beginning right. There's more to it." She could tell the look on her face would lead him to explain further. She was shocked when he seemed to drop the subject and leave the room.

"ICE CREAM!" he shouted and he re-entered a few moments later. "I think it is time for some homemade ice cream. We haven't had the homemade stuff for awhile now. What do you think dear?" he questioned as he looked at his wife. "Fine that's settled", he said as Becca's grandmother nodded her head giving a crooked smile as she glanced at Becca.

When the ice cream was ready, they all sat down with their bowls. Gramps brought in the tub of fresh made cream and filled Becca's bowl full of vanilla flavored cream. He stood beside her and waited for her to say something. She wasn't sure what he wanted her to say and she did ask, "Gramps, aren't you and Grams going to have some ice cream, too?" He said, "Oh yes. Be right back." He exited the kitchen and came back in with another tub of blueberry ice cream. He filled his bowl and his wife's bowl and Grams commented to him how delicious it was. At that point Becca spoke up and said, "Gramps, why didn't you let me know there was blueberry? Vanilla's good but blueberry has more texture and flavor. You know how much better it is."

"Just that something that really makes it good to the soul, huh?" Gramps said as he slid a spoonful of blueberry ice cream into his mouth."

"Well yeah. Why wouldn't you want *me* to enjoy something that is obviously so good to you?" Becca replied with jealousy in her voice.

Gramps looked her square in the eye and responded, "I didn't say I didn't want you to have something more than vanilla. But, as you alluded to earlier, there is nothing wrong with just enjoying the basics of something. As long as you can enjoy the benefits of the basics, what's the need to go to the trouble to add the other stuff right? Hense, I filled your bowl with the basic—*vanilla*. Me, I enjoy the stuff that makes it more pleasing to the pallet, even though it does take more work to get it there."

That day, she had never really forgotten that story. Even though she had pushed it way down inside of her, she knew right then and there that this was the reason she had always preferred any flavor over vanilla.

Suddenly her mind fast forwarded to a time when her grandfather had been in the hospital. At the time she had no idea that this would be the last visit she would make home while he was still alive. She had never experienced anyone being so seriously ill before. The assumed as she started remembering how lightly she had taken his illness was due to the lack of knowledge she had regarding his illness. She hadn't been in touch for some time with any of her family, until one evening while she lay awake listening to the sounds of the city where she then lived.

She recalled the phone ringing and deciding whether or not she should answer it. It had been so long since she had talked with any of her family, it hadn't crossed her mind that it would be her grandmother calling so late at night. She waited until the answering machine picked up.

Even as her own voice delivering her recorded apologies of not being able to come to the phone came across the speaker, she had rolled over to hug her pillow only wanting to find closure to what had been an exhausting day. She didn't want to prolong the day into the evening hours.

All of her days since moving to the city had been exhausting and unfulfilling. She had never achieved her dreams of becoming important in any way, shape or form. She had avoided contacting her family and friends in her hometown for over two years, since her last and only visit, to avoid being told, "I told you so" by anyone. She already felt like a failure. She didn't want or need anyone else telling her what she already knew.

She was certain that whoever was calling had gotten a wrong number, as was often the case. She saw no need to disrupt the misery she had slowly sank into for something that was of no importance to her.

She closed her eyes and she began her nightly ritual of crying until she fell asleep. She was interrupted by the familiar voice of her Grams as she began to leave a message. "Becca, I know it is late dear and I hate to wake you at this hour, but if you can hear me over your machine, it is very important that you pick up. It is about your grandfather. He is not well and he really wants to see you if possible. Call me as soon as you can. It took me forever to find someone who had your phone number. Please call me back".

She quickly rolled over and picked up the phone, but it was too late. Grams had already hung up. She threw some clothes and toiletries in a bag after she rushed to get dressed and headed down the elevator toward her car. She drove the remainder of the night to the only hospital close to where she had grown up.

The sun was just beginning to come up as she entered the hospital room. As she walked over to the beside she could hardly recognize the man lying there as her Gramps in the faint light coming through the blind. She remembered him being quite heavy set with a round face. She stepped out into the hallway and stopped a nurse to make sure she had the right room before waking him up.

She turned the small light over the sink area in the room before leaning over the bed rail to awaken him. "Gramps, wake up, it's Becca. I got Gram's message during the night. She said you wanted to see me, so I drove the rest of the night to get here as soon as I could." There was a long pause filled with silence. Becca started to worry. "Gramps, can you hear me?" she said as a tear rolled down her cheek.

Slowly her Gramps opened his eyes and began to rub them. "Becca, is that you, dear?" His voice was so faint. He was so weak. "Yes Gramps, it's me", she replied as she smiled at him.

He had fallen back to sleep while she held his hand and gently stroked his forehead. She sat in the chair beside the bed. She felt guilt take over her body and she stared at him only finding small glimpses that made her recognize who he was.

She smiled in the dim light of dawn when thinking about all the times he had played softball with her and how they would always sit on the porch during a thunderstorm counting the seconds between the lightening and the thunder that was to follow. She remembered how safe she felt in his arms as the lightening grew brighter and the thunder grew louder. Even when the thunder seemed to rumble her chest from its strength, she never doubted her safety while turning her head into his chest. As long as his arms were around her, she just knew she was safe.

As she sat at his bedside, she thought how wonderful it was to see him smile at her again.

She suddenly realized that he would want her to explain why she had changed so. He would notice the difference in her. He would notice her disappointment with how life had treated her. He would notice the discontentment she had with herself. She knew that he would notice, more than that, her having no joy. He would notice her again feeling alone just as she had as a small child.

After a short time she heard his voice coming from the past, "If you feel like God has left you *and* you are all alone, *you* have forgotten His promise, I will *never* leave you or forsake you. He did not leave you. He is still here. *You* have left Him." She shook this thought out of her head as the hospital seemed to come alive with noises in the early morning. She had been glad at the time, that the noises took her mind away from the past.

Becca began to drift back into a very light sleep as her mind began to go over the talks they had over his last few days of her grandfather's life. During the times alone she spent with him, she remembered how hard it had been telling him the events that lead up to her changing from the girl he so adored, and the teenager that believed in everything that he believed in, to the woman who now believed she had *little* to believe in.

Chapter 9

Fragmented memories plagued her mind about the events she shared with her grandfather in his last days. As they slowly emerged into her consciousness, she could feel herself re-experiencing the confusion, the guilt, and the hurt associated with each memory of her past.

Now, she finally realized, all the memories she had thought she had successfully managed to run from—all of the misery and unhappiness these events caused—she had ran, but she had not escaped.

She had moved to a tiny apartment upon leaving home. There was one tiny room, hardly big enough for a love seat after placing her nineteen inch television her father had given her for a going away present. She had purchased a small, flat table which was hardly big enough to place the television on from the thrift store at the end of her block. She used most of the money she had saved, which she had earned from babysitting jobs in high school, in purchasing the small things she knew she would need.

Along with the table for the television she also had purchased a long, thin table which she had placed beside the love seat, to use as an end table. She had brought along the touch light she had used in her bedroom for several years while at home. She was excited she had found a pair of barely used sheers to use on the one long, slim window in her living room as curtains. It was small, to say the least, but the touch of yellow flowers which were scattered about on the sheers gave the room a warm feeling.

She placed her kitchen table not more than three steps behind the loveseat. Her grandmother had given her a drop side table with two chairs which could not only be used as a place to eat, but could also double for a place to work on various writing projects. She thought how nice that her grandmother had thrown into the box with the table a linen covering. She smiled as she pulled it from the box, realizing that it, too, had light yellow flowers which matched, at least it somewhat matched the sheers she had hung for curtains in that room. She cleverly decided to plug the touch lamp on the end table into the electric plug which conveniently was situated between the end table and the table that would double for a work table.

Directly beside the living area, she unpacked four dishes with apples painted on the edges of the plates, four glass drinking cups that matched the dishes, having apples painted around the upper edge, four plastic bowls, six forks, six spoons, six butter knives, and two cutting knives.

Next she unpacked two spatulas, two frying pans, two pots, two lids, one spatter cover, and a few groceries her Dad and grandmother placed in her car before she left.

There had barely been enough room in the two upper cabinets and the two lower cabinets for the dishes and bowls. She had to place what silverware and cooking utensils in the one drawer the apartment provided. She had wanted more pots and pans before leaving, but was glad she hadn't brought more with her upon realizing what she had brought filled the lower cabinet and there was no more room.

She smiled upon finding a small package containing one drying towel and one dish cloth with nothing less printed on them than apples. There was no rack for hanging this extra surprise from her grandmother, so she hung the drying cloth on the handle of the cabinet directly beside the single sink and the draped the dish cloth over the kitchen faucet. Upon inspection after unpacking and situating her quaint little kitchen, she smiled again at the thought of her grandmother being so thoughtful. How could she have known that that small dish cloth and drying towel would pull together such a dreary area. She had been certain up until that point that the tiny refrigerator along with an economy stove and single sink would never look like home.

Directly behind the table she would use her work table to stack her clothes before putting them away. She neatly hung most of them in the shallow, unlit closet. As she hung them, she sorted them by categories—work clothes, dress clothes, casual wear, jackets, sweaters. She left the spring and summer wear in the box she had moved them in and tucked it into the corner. She then unpacked her shoes and placed them also by categories on top of the box.

She arranged the remainder of her things within the dresser and nightstand which the previous tenant had left behind after making sure from the landlord that the furniture would stay.

She put simple white sheets and a light, solid blue cover on the bed that the last tenants had left along with the dresser and nightstand then quickly proceeded to finish her unpacking.

She placed her battery operated, crystal lamp which was shaped like a snowman on the night stand after checking the batteries to ensure they still worked. She unpacked her Bible which had the bookmark still between the pages from the last time she had read from it. Next, she placed her alarm clock on the night stand as well, plugged it into the electric plug and set the time. She remembered feeling as if she had no reason to set the time for the alarm for the next morning.

The whole process of unpacking couldn't have taken any longer than a couple of hours. As she looked back on not having to set the alarm, she realized that was the beginning of the following feelings of having no hope.

The remainder of the afternoon, she ran to the grocery store just a few doors down from her apartment and purchased a pound of hamburger, some Hamburger Helper, a few potatoes and an ear of corn. She stopped by the newspaper vendor stand to purchase a paper to look for a part time job the next day.

After having dinner and feeling quite lost, she laid in her new bed staring at the lit snowman until she fell asleep.

Chapter 10

The next couple of weeks were filled for Becca. She consumed every moment of her time looking for a job. The only time she could remember smiling during that time was at the simple things that reminded her of home. She had grown up in a simple time. Every time she looked at her apple patterned dishes, she thought of her grandmother.

As she explained these things to her grandfather as he lay there in the hospital, she realized how the simple things had lost their meaning to her.

Her mind skipped ahead to a different day, trying to convince her grandfather she was justified in why she had changed her views and convictions. She had found an evening job at a diner which was just around the corner from the small but quaint apartment which reminded her so much of home. She found herself anxiously waiting for her shift to begin. So much so, that she volunteered to take the midnight shift—on top of the dinner shift she already had. Since she knew no one in the city, the interaction with the customers was a welcome escape from the silence she experienced at home in her tiny apartment, having no one to talk to.

Slowly she had started, at least somewhat, of a relationship with several of the repeat customers at the diner. She listened, although not intentionally, to situations and problems in their lives while serving them. Occasionally one of them would ask her opinion about one matter or another. It didn't take her long before she was feeling completely and utterly alone in the world she had created for herself by shutting everyone she knew out of her life.

While conveying her story to her grandfather, she couldn't help but suppress the agonizing feeling that she had done the absolute wrong thing by shutting everyone out. But, by this time in her life, she had become especially good at suppressing her feelings and reasoning things away in order to justify things to herself.

After what was the usual amount of time for a stranger who encounters people they are in contact with on a daily basis, some of the customers started asking her about things in her life.

She realized by the conversations she had overheard concerning their lives that her life was quite dull in comparison. This had made the temptation of embellishing certain facts, and for lack of a better term, to just downright lie, too easy to resist. After all, no one really knew her. She could explain away the fact of her working in a diner by telling them she had came from a wealthy family, but most of what they had, had been squandered away by a controlling sibling following the horrible accident her parents had died in when she was younger.

She knew her grandfather was disappointed in her by the way he only glanced at her as she was speaking. Until that moment, she hadn't thought much about the consequences of her lies once they came out into the light. She could tell by her grandfather's moistened eyes how much it hurt him for her to be so ashamed of her family and how she was raised—how much she must have been ashamed of him and her grandmother even thought they had always been there for her.

Lying in her bed, going back through this conversation, she knew she had been wrong in denying the ones who had done so much for her.

The deafening silence that followed after admitting the truth to her grandfather regarding the truth she had created for herself, was as strong as the silence she felt alone in the darkness of her room. She remembered feeling as if she had been let off the hook when the silence was broken by a nurse entering the hospital room to check her grandfather's vital signs and to administer pain medication.

She would not realize until long after the conversation with her grandfather was over and he had been gone for some time, that this had actually been the beginning of her realization she had not only deceived everyone around her with her lies, but she had in fact let her own lies become a horrible deception to herself. She would not know that once her web of deception was brought into the light, the light would only get brighter as time went by.

The next morning she avoided any mention of trying to continue her story. Even when asked by her grandfather to continue on, she was reluctant about doing so. She had no choice but to continue when he let her know he had asked the nurse to not allow any visitors until 6:00 in the evening in order to have no interruptions. The only exceptions would be the ones from the nurses and aids to check his vitals and administer medications. She then continued down the path she had headed the day before.

A few months into her job at the diner, one of her favorite repeat customers, Mary, whom always waited until one of Becca's tables had become available to be seated, invited her to come to a gathering at her home. Mary had always left her a generous tip. Mary thought it would give her a chance to make some connections and enable her to further her career in another direction.

She shared how she somewhat felt that Mary had offered out of feeling sorry for her. But, since she needed all the help she could get, she decided to accept Mary's invitation.

Mary was extremely polite. She was in her mid twenties and was always dressed in bright, cheerful clothing. She was always smiling and laughing. She could tell by the grooming of her hair and nails that she was from a family who was well off. Even when Mary wasn't at the diner, the other customers were always asking if she had been there and she was part of their conversation in one way or another.

For the first time since working at the diner, she asked for a night off. Mary expected her at Mary's beach house at nine o'clock for an after swim party dinner. She had been nervous all day about the outfit she was going to wear to the gathering and wondering what to expect. As she drove past the address Mary had given her, she was definitely out of her comfort zone. The homes and the cars were like nothing she had ever seen before. It was as if the whole community came right out of a magazine. Suddenly her apartment seemed small and insignificant. She passed Mary's house embarrassed to pull in the drive way with her small, second hand car. Finally she convinced herself that the lies she had told to everyone about her past would make everyone overlook her present financial condition.

After taking a deep breath, she walked up the gigantic, multi-level, granite steps and rang the doorbell. At that point she had decided not to ever invite any of her new found friends to her tiny, closet sized apartment.

Her grandfather was letting her do all the talking. He hid his emotions very well, or so it seemed to her. Occasionally she could catch a hint of an expression that seemed as though he was sympathetic to her journey or at least what she had decided to share with him so far.

She continued over the remaining length of his illness to pull facts that she thought he would find compassion for. In doing so, she was trying to gain an ally that would confirm she was justified in all the things she had done that led her so far away from the ones who cared so deeply for her.

She decided to stay at the hospital over the next several nights. She wanted to be there as much as she could. Her grandfather had taken a turn for the worse in his condition. He was sleeping more and his pain had increased. This gave her less and less time to build an ally in him.

Becca had believed at the time she was sharing her experience with her grandfather was for his benefit but while going in and out of sleep and focusing on the tiny shiver of light that had worked it's way into her room she realized that in reality it was done so only to benefit herself.

Each time her grandfather awoke, he would hold off as long as he possibly could to further rest just to be able to hear more of her story. She continued on each time he gestured for her to do so.

Becca shared how one of her friends had a family member who was not as well off as the rest of her family. They had asked Becca to sit with her, giving their family members a much needed break of taking care of her. It was something that she had found herself really enjoying and it helped her to be able to afford more things in life. She had even been able to purchased a lake front house so the trip wouldn't be so far each day.

She was spending less and less time at her home on the lake and more and more time at the luxurious homes of her friends who lived in more affluent neighborhoods. She had replaced all of the simple things that once brought her joy with more expensive articles. She attended parties and rubbed elbows with gentlemen that showered her with expensive jewelry and constant gifts.

She explained away the relationships with many different men. She justified never being in a relationship long because sooner or later something would happen that she just wasn't satisfied with. She thought she deserved more than what she was getting out of the relationship and too much was expected out of her. Her mind returned to the presence time and the bitter truth that she was now all alone.

Becca wondered if part of the reason she kept going over her past in her mind was because she was so alone with no one to share her life with, or if it was because she was going insane.

At a tender moment when she let her guard down she wondered how she could have ever been ashamed of her family and where she had come from. Then her heart would harden once again and return to thinking she still deserved more as she drifted back into a light sleep.

In her sleep she could hear the sound of her grandmother's voice greeting her in the hallway of the hospital as she arrived late the next evening. Her grandfather was getting worse. It would be just a matter of time before nature would take its course. Tears streamed down her grandmother's face as she broke the news to her. Although she knew she should comfort her grandmother, she stiffened up and excused herself from the conversation while making excuses about why she needed to leave.

She waited until visiting hours were over to return to the hospital. By then her grandfather was very weak. The nurse asked her to let him rest which would enable him to save his strength for later. That night there was silence. Neither of the two spoke. She would smile at him when he woke up and he would smile in return. Once again she was relieved thinking their intense conversation had ended.

Chapter 11

Becca's grandfather, although very weak, woke up in the middle of the night. She was in a deep sleep when she was awakened by his voice calling out to her. Rubbing her eyes, she stumbled over to his bed. He motioned to her, letting her know he wanted her to move her chair closer to his bed. After doing so, he began his response to the story she had shared with him over the past several nights.

At first, she told him that he should not try to talk and asked him to save his strength.

Regardless of her request, he would not keep silent. He rolled himself to the edge of the bed, nestling himself against the guard rails. His voice was faint. In return she slid her chair as close as possible. She positioned herself so she could rest her arm on the rails and laid her head on it and listened intently to his words.

"Becca, as you probably already know or you can imagine that I am not very pleased at what you have told me. I have listened to you without interrupting. Now, I expect you to do the same for me while I say what I have to say to you." She could tell by the serious tone in his voice that she was getting ready to be put into her place. She looked into his eyes as she simply nodded her head and replied, "Go ahead Grampa. I probably deserve whatever you have to say to me."

As she was speaking, she couldn't help notice that his countenance had changed. His eyes were wide open. The light which escaped from the partially opened bathroom door played around his head. His silver hair was shinning as if there was a glow emitting from him. His eyes were full of color—more vibrant blue than she had ever seen them before. His words were so sure with a certainty she had never heard from him before. He spoke with authority.

"Becca, you have always been one who thought you deserved more than what you have had. I remember your sixth birthday. What a fit you threw in the store over the bike you wanted.

You had no clue that your father had taken you there for me. I was in the back of the store watching and waiting to find out which bike you would pick out. I knew your father could not afford a new bike at that time, so I had decided I would purchase the bike for you as an early birthday present—since I would not be in town for your birthday party to give it to you in person. After witnessing the fit you threw and seeing your father have to carry you out of the store, I didn't purchase it. I knew in my heart that if I had bought it that day, you would have thought that you gained it by your own merits. You would have thought that throwing a fit for it was why you got it. In other words, my dear Becca, you were not ready to have it even though I was ready and eager to give it to you. I wanted to give it to you simply because you wanted it and I loved you. It wasn't because you deserved it or had earned it. I simply wanted to express my love to you. The way you reacted in the store left me with no other choice than to forfeit the idea of buying you the bike. To have given in, in reaction to your temper tantrum, would have lead you to overlook that love was the reason for the gift. Sometimes we confuse wanting something for deserving something. I was hoping by holding things back from you when you were rebellious would teach you how God withholds some things from us when we are rebellious with Him. I thought that you had learned this lesson before you became an adult. God knows when *we are not ready* for some things and waits to give them until He knows we are."

After that he drifted back into a deep sleep that would not last for long.

She closed her eyes as she remembered his words. "I never realized you were trying to teach me a lesson. I never realized God deals with us the same way", was the last thought that went through her mind before she, too, had drifted into a deep sleep alongside her grandfather.

Becca set up in her bed and could feel the fan as it moved from side to side of her room.

She hadn't realized she had fallen asleep again in her own home. She was startled. It was getting hard for her to distinguish her past memories from her present. Feeling as if she had been asleep for days, she checked her clock once more. "I must be caught in a time glitch", she said as she shook her head. Hardly any time had passed since she last checked the time. It seemed that each memory was stacked on top of the other—flooding her mind. Somehow she was able to sift through each one in unison and process each simultaneously.

Her memory turned again to the hospital room and her grandfather's words. As she pulled the sheet over her shoulders as she slipped back down in the bed and laying her on her pillow, she felt as if she were a young child again being tucked into bed as she her grandfather's words flooded her mind.

"God knows our wants and all of our needs. He always supplies our needs He is eager to give us our wants and desires. Many times He holds the things we desires back until we are willing to see that it was not by any thing we did by which we earned or deserved them. God knows we are not ready to receive things sometimes."

"We wouldn't know how to handle having them, but more than that God knows when we are not capable of handling losing them. This explains why some work hard all their life and it seems as though they gain the world and others work hard and can barely make ends meet. That's not to say that is the only reason that situations happen, but just one of the reasons."

"At times, holding things back from us is what God sees as one of our necessities. He sees and knows so much more than we could ever imagine. Of course, we don't understand how He works because we will never have the inside information He does. It doesn't make sense for us to even try to understand His ways. That is another mistake we make. We don't have the capacity to have even the slightest inkling of understanding compared to His. If we did, I believe, we would never question Him or blame Him for anything,"

Becca was trying hard to understand what she her memory had brought back to her. Her grandfather's words, so clear, but seeming to be a mystery yet somehow was beginning to make sense to her—little by little. In the faintest of voices these words escaped from her mouth: "Did my grandfather just say that all people are ignorant in spite of all of our education, accomplishments, and experiences?" She sat up in her bed once more and began again to hear her grandfather's words:

"We, Becca, are intelligent as our brain will allow. But, God is so much more than we are.

If we could understand all of His reasons for doing things the way He does, we would be God.

That is another mistake we make. We fail miserably by thinking we are in control of anything.

Nothing is given and nothing is gained except that God gives it. Even when we are so caught up in our own lives and totally disregard Him, He brings good things into our lives to bring us happiness. He gives us others to help us, to love us, to share things with. He gives us material possessions we desire, good jobs, great friends, good times to store in our memories. All of these things are not because we made them happen, but because God put is in the position to be able to have them. God's grace is so perfect, that He gives good things all the time—whether we realize it or not."

"As far as giving up on relationships because you don't get as much as you think you deserve from the other person, remember Becca, that God never gives up in His relationship with us—even though he deserves much more than our best that we can possibly give him. We fall short sometimes. No let me rephrase that, we fall short of what He deserves all of the time."

"I often wonder how you used to come to the conclusion how you deserved things. What is the measure you use in deciding whether someone has let you down and you decide to give up on that relationship? What is the measure and the amount of time you use to determine that the other person is deserving for you to *not* give up on them in a relationship?"

"What is the measure you compare to that lets you know you deserve more than what you are getting from a relationship? What is the measure you compare to that lets you know you have fallen short of to know you do *not* deserve more than what you are getting from that relationship?"

"Chances are that you have no real or stable measure to compare these things to and the way you measure it results from how you "*feel*" at the moment. The measure never stays the same.

It is constantly changing. It is a measure no one can satisfy because they never know from one moment to the next what the degree of the measurement you are using is. The probability that other people in your relationships are using the same way of measuring as you are is extremely high. How could anyone expect to ever have a lasting relationship under these circumstances?"

As Becca lay in her bed, she thought back over all the relationships in her life. The people she had pushed away, the harsh words she had used with one's that she knew had loved her so dearly. She had run away from everyone who had tried to help her, and to guide her for no real reason. She knew her grandfather's words were true. The only thought in her mind was, "Please memory don't fail me now. Please help me to remember if my grandfather told me the answer to this endless cycle of running away from and pushing away everyone who cared about me."

As she laid there exhausted, staring once again at the fragment of light that had snuck into her room, her grandfather's words continued.

"God doesn't look at love the same way you do, Becca. Deserving His love isn't even a part of His love for us. We may think God falls short on how we measure how He loves us, but because we can't comprehend all He knows and sees, we can't see with our eyes or tell by our feelings the truth—that He never falls short in His love for us."

"God asks us to strive and to try to do our very best to the best of our ability to love Him and to love each other the way He loves us. He expects us to fall short. He expects us to give Him less than He deserves from us. But, His love for us is so perfect that it is able to overcome our short comings. He expects us to realize that when we do fall short to know that He will continue to love us. *This, Becca, is the kind of love He wants us to have for one another!*"

"Becca, I don't believe we deserve anything from God because even if we mess up just once, that makes us unworthy of His love. Let's face it, Becca, no matter who you are or where you or from or what your background is, we all mess up at least once. But, nonetheless, He still loves us. He keeps giving us chance after chance after chance to accept His love—regardless of how many times we mess up. You'd be hard pressed to find any one of us who is that tolerant when it comes to giving our love."

"Loving someone has nothing to do with how much we perceive the other person loves us.

Regardless of how much another does for us or gives us has really nothing to do with us loving them. If it does, it is not really us loving them, but rather us accepting their love for us. When we love another, it is to be done because of something inside of ourselves that enables us to find the commitment to do so—even when they mess up. Real love involves knowing you care for the welfare of another and desiring to make them happier by adding to or enriching their life. Once you learn how to do that, love flows from another to you naturally. It makes the other in the relationship to begin to put you first, before themselves—before their wants and desires."

"This kind of love comes from God. Once you realize how much He loves you, only then can you love someone else in a way that isn't selfish. If someone else loves you in this manner, it is because Goad has filled them with the capacity to do so. Once again this is the perfect grace that God gives to even those who repeatedly reject His love."

"If what you desire in a relationship is things and possessions from the other to prove to you their love for you, then nothing will ever grow from it. You will always find something you can use to push you away and make you run. Remember, Becca, it is your love for them that makes you stay and work through the hard times—not what they do for you."

"I pray for you, Becca. My time is short in this world. Promise me that when I am gone that you will take the time to not just look at things in a fleeting manner. Watch, think about my passing and what is left when all is said and done. If you do, you may just see what life *really* boils down to."

Chapter 12

Becca remembered awakening in her chair beside her grandfather's bed the following morning in the hospital room. Her hand had drifted in her sleep onto the bedding while she had rested her head on the railing and had fallen asleep. Sometime during the early morning hours, her grandfather had slipped his hand around hers. As her eyes adjusted to the light of the early morning sun peeking through the window, she realized her grandfather had slipped away and was gone. She remembered the nurse stepping up behind her and taking her by the hand to lead her outside into the hallway.

Becca felt numb. She questioned, "How could I have fallen asleep when I knew he was so weak? How could I have let him talk to me so long knowing it would weaken him even more?"

Becca's thoughts turned to her grandmother who had not yet arrived.

Becca walked outside to wait for her grandmother to arrive, knowing that the hospital was contacting her with the news of her grandfather dying.

Complete and utter silence filled the air. A few small sparrows flew overhead. In slow motion, Becca raised her gaze into the sky. Sunrise was approaching. The morning sun had just begun to brighten the sky. Colors of red and grey drew her into a trance. The sun continued to rise over the horizon as she stood there waiting. Rays of sun broke through the clouds in ribbons of silk through the thick morning dew. The grass shimmered as the light danced from one droplet of moisture to another. How beautiful the morning was, even on such a heart breaking day.

Becca had managed to avoid her father so far. She didn't think she could face him. He had been abandoned all those years ago by her mother, his wife, and she knew how hard it had been on him. He had never gone on with his life really. It was if he had spent all those years wrapped up in pain—waiting for her to return, knowing the whole time that she never would. She had seen his misery and saw the pain in his eyes, year after year, of loving someone so much and losing them. She thought to herself, "How can I face him? I have done the same thing causing him so much more pain and anguish." She wondered how he would react when she finally saw him. Even more she wondered what her actions would be. Just as the little girl who had been left at her grandmother's when he went on a business trip, she knew deep down inside, that she wanted to just into his arms and tell him how sorry she was.

Becca's grandmother had promised she would not say a word to her father that she was there. She had kept it a secret from him so far and somehow Becca managed to elude him, even at the hospital. She knew that he would be at the funeral because even though her grandfather was the father of the woman who had hurt him so badly, they all always been as close as father and son themselves.

At the funeral, Becca waited for all that would attend the funeral to arrive before she drove to the graveside. Her father was standing next to her grandmother. Becca hesitated, seeing him there, before opening the car door and making herself known. As she neared the two, who were now arm in arm, she took a deep breath, stepped from behind her father and silently gave him a hug. He spoke no words but instead gently slipped his hand into hers. As she looked at him, a tear escaped from the corner of his eye as he looked at her and slowly nodded his head.

It seemed as though the whole town was there—Mr. Simon, her high school math teacher; Dr. Elbert, whom she had known since birth; Bobbie, the butcher at the local grocery store were all in attendance. Others she knew whom she could not recall their names had also taken time out of their day to pay their respects. Becca remembered them all except for one young gentleman that no one seemed to recognized, at least no one acknowledged knowing him—no one except her grandmother. As Becca stare at him from a distance, there was something familiar about him—something that drew her to him.

After the funeral Becca questioned her grandmother as to whom this young man was that no one else seemed to know but her. Her grandmother acted as if she had not heard her inquiry and changed the subject to something else.

Becca knew that her grandmother's avoidance of the subject was not in her grandmother's character. Becca wondered to herself, "What was her grandmother hiding?"

In an instant, Becca remembered that in the days just after her grandfather's passing, going through his belongings with her grandmother. Conversation between the two of them had been scarce during the process of doing so.

A yard sale was planned for all of her grandfather's personal possessions. They were neatly lined up on tables and placed neatly. His favorite Sunday clothes were folded to perfection and his shoes set beside each suit he had worn them with. His tools, razors, music collection, radios, a CB radio he had received as a gift on Christmas, books, coin collection, comic book collection and baseball cards he had cherished as a boy were spaced in a manner which made them easily seen.

Becca remembered taking a great deal of time to arrange all his things. They used such care. Memories swamped Becca's mind as they handled all his things. At times, she had not wanted to loosen her grip on articles to place them for the sale. "Oh, how he had loved some of these things", she said as the last item was placed for display. This was the hardest thing she had ever had to do.

The morning of the sale, she showed up early. No one else was there except her grandmother when she arrived. As they took one last look at all her grandfather's articles, her grandmother broke the silence. "Becca, don't get too caught up in possessions here on earth. This is what it all boils down to when you put your security in material things."

Becca looked at her grandmother with the question of "why" being evident on her face.

Her grandmother placed her hand on her shoulder and continued her thought as Becca stood there not being able to say a single word.

"All these things, although as treasured as they were by your grandfather, in the end they are all just second hand items that others are only willing to pay next to nothing for."

As these words flooded Becca's mind, she knew that her grandfather had prepared a lesson for her. All her life she had been obsessed with "things"—material things, symbolic gestures. Her grandmother was right, in the end they don't seem to amount to much at all.

She remembered that during the entirety of the sale of her grandfather's things how hoards of on lookers and those who had just stopped out of curiosity responded in one of two ways. They either picked through them like vultures, taking from here and leaving from there, or simply walking by as if his possessions were not worth having.

Becca sat up in her bed with a sense of humility and humbleness. She turned the light on which sat on the table next to her bed. She took mental inventory of all her belongings; her gold jewelry, some with precious stones. She thought about her china, her silver, several pieces of antique furniture, expensive shoes in her closet she had bought while living in the city, her Mercedes in the driveway and an original painting a gentleman friend had purchased for her at an auction. None of these things seemed like much to her at the moment when she realized that some day it would be her things that others would pick apart or simply walk right by.

Becca's room was now filling with light. The tiny streak of light she had stared at until this point was fading with a new influx of light from her lamp. She couldn't help but wonder if somehow the tiny streak of light was likened to a tiny bit of light inside of her that had been flickering inside her own personal darkness which had over taken her very being. She wondered if somehow that tiny flicker could turn into part of a much brighter light.

Becca glanced at her clock. Her eyes opened wide with surprise how little time had gone by since she had gone to bed when compared to all she had relived during the night. So many memories had come back to her in such a small amount of time. She turned off the light as she lay back down resting her head on a partially elevated pillow. Somehow she knew that there was much further to go before the flicker of light inside of her would turn into a brilliant light that no darkness could put out.

Chapter 13

After falling into a light sleep, she felt her subconscious going back to when she was a teenager. The feeling she was experiencing was sereal at times. She remembered thinking to herself that she had forgotten so much and there was so much she had never realized. She had gone back in time. A time where the feeling of being insignificant, small, meaningless, being overlooked for who she was. The feeling that everything that was important to her was unimportant to anyone else. The feeling was overwhelming.

Becca's mind was being flooded simultaneously with disappointments she experienced as a teenager. In her sleep, in her dream, she sensed she was not alone in her room. She felt no fear from whoever or whatever was there with her. Her mind jumped to different stages of her life in a instant—times she had struggled through while transitioning from a child to young adulthood to womanhood—times she had felt all alone.

She was thirteen and had been invited to go to the movies with several of her friends. Mad and throwing things in her room, she was shouting loudly so that her father could hear her through the walls. She remembered intentionally trying to hurt him with her words—just like she was hurt by not being allowed to go. She heard her own voice of thirteen screaming, "It's not fair. No one cares about me and what I need. All they care about is what they want. Wait until the next time someone wants something from me. We'll see how they like it when I refuse giving them what they want."

The picture of herself in her room as a teenager froze in her mind as though it was a snapshot someone had taken while hiding in her room all those years ago.

Her mind was now playing tricks on her. She wasn't able to tell if she was in a dream or in the present time. She faintly heard a voice speaking to her. "Becca", was the only thing could make out. She turned quickly and only caught a glimpse of a shadow she didn't recognize. Still not sure if she was awake or sleeping, the voice revealed itself once again. "What were you doing, Becca?"

Becca knew the voice but still couldn't quite put her finger on who she was remembering now. Even though she had difficulty knowing who it was, she answered. "Just blowing off steam" she scarcely replied. "I was young and felt like I wasn't being treated fairly. I deserved to go to the movie with my friends" Becca answered sharply.

"Why do you answer so harshly before you know why I was asking you the question about what you were doing? How do you know that I wasn't already sympathetic to your experience?"

"I don't know" Becca replied, now in a softer voice. "I assume it is just a defense mechanism."

"Defense mechanism? Or is it a barrier to hide your true feelings behind? Maybe a way to hide fear of a misconceived notion you had to defend yourself against? Maybe perhaps something used to control others into fearing they would not be found in your good graces?" The voice now sounding a little smug itself—almost with a tone of humor mocking her.

"I have found that every time throughout your life when you haven't gotten your way, you react with *your* self—described *defense mechanism*. That tactic can be used in order to achieve or at least make others react the way you think they should act. The problem is, if you react that way in every situation that you don't get your way, you never know the response you will get because of how you may or may not be perceived. It doesn't ensure you will get what you want at all. But, there's one thing for sure, everyone else will definitely know what to expect from you and how you will react all the time. At least they won't get any surprises from you. Once they learn how you are, they know no matter what they do, if you're not happy with it, they would give us trying to get a different reaction from you. Sounds more like you are giving others opportunity to push your buttons and have more of a way to control you. Especially if you change your expectations or desires concerning what you expect from them in how they react in situations. Let's face it Becca, you do that all the time."

Becca could feel resent rising as the voice sounded even more sarcastic than before.

"Although, I guess in some ways you would always know what to expect from others. I mean you could be certain that everyone would eventually give up on trying to make you happy."

After a long pause, the voice continued, "Isn't that what you are trying to achieve with your defense mechanism? On the other hand, seeing as you always desiring others to stay in your live, it couldn't possibly be that . . ."

After another short pause the voice once again broke the silence. "Yes that is it. You've always felt like you deserved for everyone to leave you just like you felt you didn't deserve any one to love you."

"Such a genius you are Becca. Finding a way to get exactly what you deserved all the time and finding a way for the blame not to be placed on you but on someone else. *Absolute genius!*"

Becca abruptly awakened and sat up in bed once again. "That can't be true . . . can it?" She was questioning herself and what she had held as her own truth. Thinking to herself, "yes", as she answered her own question, she knew she had to exam the self truth she had created for herself as part of her defense mechanism.

This revelation left Becca totally wiped out and reeling with emotion. She found herself begging for peace, for rest—for her soul to be still.

As Becca drifted off lightly she remembered the voice of the woman whom she had thought was in her room. A woman her father had hired to stay with her while he was away on a business trip—a woman she had given a hard time from the day she arrived until the day she left.

She hadn't wanted her to stay there because she thought she was old enough to stay by herself.

Her father had thought differently at the time. He didn't want to worry while he was away what was going on at home, especially since her grandmother wasn't able to have her over since she was out of town herself what her grandmother called "her mystery trip." The woman she despised so much at the time had managed to ream her out with words she had just relived before her father had come back home.

Chapter 14

Within all the memories that were flooding Becca's mind was the suppression of something deeper. It was aware there was something stronger and devastating locked deep down inside of her—something so painful—a memory that could not come out until she faced the voices and memories which lay on the surface. She would not be ready or able to deal with what had devastated her so many years ago until God had gotten her to a place of acceptance, forgiveness and repentance. A memory which would affect her entire life forever—buried along with a mystery that she was now convinced existed—which would explain what had caused her to separate herself emotionally from everyone in her life.

Becca longed for healing. She longed for the closeness she knew she had felt as a tiny child—the closeness that was a result of much more than having her mother in her life. There was something else missing that had been ripped away from her leaving her empty. She didn't know what it could be, but it had been strong enough to distract her from the small amount of faith she had as a teenager.

Becca had lived her entire life afraid of the awareness of a memory that she had let cause so many failed relationships and bad decisions. She needed to allow this "thing" to surface—whatever it was, regardless of the pain involved. In her heart she asked God to help her to remember. As she asked God for His help, she once again remembered her grandfather's words, "Sometimes God holds those things back that we ask for because he knows we are not able to handle them."

Becca pulled the cover up around her neck for the first time since moving to this heat drenched town. She heard the tapping of rain on her bedroom window begin, but did not stir. Her mind had gone blank for the first time since going to bed in what seemed to be an eternity ago.

Becca's eyes were heavy. She could tell they were swollen from the restless night she had experienced thus far.

Becca awakened to the sound of raindrops which had become more intense and realized she had left her windows up. She grabbed her robe and stumbled through the house closing them one by one.

The presence of calmness was now apparent within her mind.

After closing the last window, Becca opened her front door and walked out onto the steps which lead down to her covered porch so she could smell the fragrance of the summer rain. She sat down on the steps and wrapped her arms around the spindles of the rails. She could hear the gentle sound of thunder in the distance slowly approaching.

Becca closed her eyes and leaned her head toward the rails she was holding. The first moment of contentment flowed over her for the first time in years. She pictured her father's face, not as she saw him at her grandfather's funeral, but as she had seen him as a small child.

Most of her life, her father had a sadness in his eyes. She could see the loss he felt. But, the father she was picturing was filled with happiness, kindness, love, contentment and joy.

A large bang sounded from the lightening as the storm drew nearer. Becca jumped from fear of the thunder and lightning as she had done as a child. In an instant, the memories began to rise once more.

In Becca's mind, she was a very young child once again. She had woken up crying in the middle of the night—frightened by the blinding flashes of light coming through the window and the rumbling of the thunder which made the whole room seem to shake.

As soon as she saw the door to her room open and her father had stepped one step inside her room, she sprang from her bed and jumped into his arms.

His arms were strong and she felt safe. He sat between the two twin beds beside her until the storm had subsided and her fear had all but gone away. He kissed her good-night and . . . Then Becca remembered something she hadn't remembered before. Her father leaned down to the other twin bed beside hers and whispered something as if someone else was in the room. His words were muffled as if something didn't want her to know what He had said.

Confusion filled her mind as she tried to figure out what she had not remembered about that night—who was in her room and what did her father say to them?

Becca returned to her bedroom and pulled the covers up to her neck again before the memory continued.

The following morning, after the storm, Becca followed the sounds she heard coming from upstairs from the breakfast table where she was sitting. She followed the sound to her bedroom.

She found her mother just finishing making her bed and turning to make the bed next to hers.

Becca, feeling shock as she lay there remembering—shocked by having a memory of her mother, but more shocked that someone had definitely slept in the bed next to her without her remembering anything about it.

Questions plagued her mind. Who was there? Why were they in her room? Why could she not remember them being there?

Finally, Becca drifted off into a deep, deep, well needed sleep.

Chapter 15

Becca was totally mentally exhausted by the time the sun began to rise. Finally finished re-living all the events that had plagued her mind, she realized it was not a fact that all the noise from the sirens, the yelling, or the train cars that had kept her sleepless and exhausted all those years. She knew that she had only thought all this time she was in control of everything in her life.

She had believed that she had total control by not confronting all the feelings she had kept hidden. Finally understanding that by doing so she had in effect given control of herself and her life over to something or someone who really had no control over anything. She had been deceived for so long.

She stumbled to the sink in her bathroom, splashed water on her face then had begun to brush her hair. Upon doing so she noticed the small streaks of grey, as the brush ran down toward the ends of her hair. She realized that a huge portion of her life had been wasted. After this one night of regrets, she was ready to give up on what for so long she thought was control.

She lay the brush down, bent down on her knees, lowered her head while covering her face with her hands and began to cry softly. She was broken from all the words she had pushed aside for so long. She could not hold back as she cried out loudly to the only One she knew that could help her. She began asking for forgiveness for turning a deaf ear all those years. As she surrendered her life to the control of another, she felt as if a huge weight had been lifted from upon her shoulders.

She finally understood that all the years she had felt like she deserved more from everyone in her life than what they had been willing to give was in vain. Getting because she felt she deserved was not what was going to give her peace. It was receiving from the One who had given everything He had for her, even giving His life and shedding His blood, to set her free from the bondage that had plagued her. It was being willing to receive what she had not deserved that would set her free.

Just then she realized it was Sunday morning. She rushed into her bedroom to check the time. It was almost ten o'clock. She rushed to her closet to find a dress that would be appropriate.

Just as she finished getting dressed, she stopped for the last time to look in the mirror to ensure she was presentable. She turned to go out the door as the bells chimed in the church steeple. She remembered about her Bible. She quickly scanned her bookshelf to find her King James which had been given to her as a child by her grandmother. She stopped to pick up a notepad and pen and headed out the door. She was filled with excitement and energy as she quickly walked down the sidewalk to catch up with Mrs. Kirby and the Callahan's.

She too was now laughing and smiling as she joined in on the highlight of the week; enjoying her first experience of going to church in this new town she now called home.

That morning, Becca kneeled at the alter at church for the first time. She asked God to help her unravel the meaning of the memory of her mother and the person who had been in her room as a child. She opened her heart and asked God to help her deal with the most painful mistake she had ever made which she had never shared with another soul.

Chapter 16

Several weeks had passed since Becca had made her most important decision. She was unaware that God had been working and a chain of events would begin to unfold that would change he life forever.

Church was letting out and Becca had walked home enjoying the beautiful fall morning.

The slight breeze in the air, the changing of the leaves to magnificent yellows, reds and oranges was breathtaking. Her mind floated away with excitement from signing up for the fall festival as a helper for the cake walk. These thoughts reminded her of her father as he had carried her in his arms when she was young while participating in the cake walk in her hometown church all those years ago.

After returning home, Becca picked up the phone and called information asking for the number to the local Inn near her home town of Statesville. She quickly called the Inn and made reservations for the following weekend. She needed to set things right with her father. It had been six years since she had seen him. She didn't want to wait a minute longer than she had to, to restore her relationship with him or to at least start mending it.

The next five days were filled with expectations of healing, laughter and starting that part of her life anew. Becca patiently waited until Friday morning and packed her things. As she headed out of her home which was now in Spring Hope she took a deep breath and headed out on her way to do what she should have done so many years ago.

Anxiety and fear of what her father's reaction would be crept inside of her. She reminded herself that "all things work together for good to those who believe." She reminded herself that she trusted God in all things and circumstances and expected to see Him work in the requests of the prayers she had made known to Him.

It wasn't long before Becca had left her home she was unpacking her bag at the Inn. She stopped for lunch on the way to her childhood home.

So many things had changed. The theater where her and her grandmother went to during their *Opportunity Times* no longer stood where it had all those years ago. "What a shame", Becca thought to herself. "I used to love sitting in the balcony watching all those Disney movies with Grams." Standing in its place was a drugstore.

There was no more play ground beside the town cemetery. She remembered playing there on Sunday mornings after church with all of her friends. Oh how she loved the bi-plane sliding board that used to sit in the middle of the park. She had loved airplanes ever since the first time she had set eyes on the slide.

One thing had not changed. Dogwoods lined every street in town. She wished it was spring so she could once again witness the adornment of the trees with their fully bloomed, beautiful white petal flowers.

She drove past the lake where she had spent endless days feeding the ducks and adoring the ducklings.

When she reached the five point intersection just past the lake, her mouth watered when her eyes caught sight of her favorite barbecue restaurant. She couldn't believe it was still there after all these years. She pulled in quickly and ordered two barbecue sandwiches with slaw to go.

She hoped her father still loved them as much as he did when she was a child.

After arriving at her father's home, she was greeted at the door by the person she least expected to see—Nicole.

Nicole beamed as she hugged her neck and greeted her. "Your father will be so excited to see you."

As she and Nicole they stepped into the living room, Nicole gently pulled her to the side and explained that there were some changes with her father that had taken place since the last time Becca had been home.

Becca was shocked and saddened to find out that her father now suffered from dementia.

Nicole took a deep breath before explaining further, "I'm not sure your father will know who you or not. He goes in and out and I never know when it will happen."

Upon entering the room, Becca sat in the chair next to her father. He acted as if no one else was in the room with him. She waited to begin to talk, not knowing what to expect.

Finally her father spoke up. It was evident that he had no clue who she was.

"Where is my son? Why did you take my son away from me?"

Not knowing what to say or do, Becca only shook her head and said, "Dad, it's me, Becca—your daughter. Don't' you remember me?"

Confusion flooded her father's face. Crying he asked again, "Please tell me where my son is. Why did you take my son?"

The next instant, he turned to stare out the windows—entering into his own world.

On the drive home, Becca asked God to give her father comfort and to heal him from his condition. She kept asking herself, "Why on earth did he think he had a son?"

Becca had been gone from home and away from her father too long. It was too late to mend things with him now.

She prayed and asked for forgiveness for her stubbornness in not going home all those years.

Chapter 17

Becca returned home to find that Mr. Jackson, Aaron, was in need of a part-time sitter to help out with his son, Jacob, in the evening and on the weekends. After being laid off from his job almost a year ago, he had now found a position which would allow him to afford hiring someone to help out. The hours varied from week to week but the pay and benefits were excellent.

Becca needed the extra money, so she was relieved when Aaron hired her to help out.

Aaron had seemed somewhat reluctant in the beginning to hire her. She thought mainly because she hadn't lived there long and he didn't know her very well except for the brief encounters at the store each morning.

Becca loved spending time with the little boy who had stolen her heart from the first day she had seen him at the store and had followed her up and down the aisles.

Little by little, Aaron started opening up to her. In the beginning she couldn't shake the idea that somehow she knew Aaron from her past.

Jacob had started depending on her more and more to spend time with him. Aaron had shared how Jacob's mother died he was only a year old.

After Jacob had gone to bed at night, Becca and Aaron would talk. Becca had usually baked a cake or pie and would fix coffee for the two of them to share while sitting on the front porch as they winded down from their day.

Aaron had told her how he and his wife had tried several years to have a child on their own, but never could and how they had adopted Jacob when he was just a few hours old.

As time went by, Aaron would stop by Becca's house on Sunday afternoons after church.

They would sit on the porch and talk while Jacob either played in the yard or watched television until it was time to get ready for Sunday night service at church.

There was a closeness that she couldn't explain that she felt between Aaron and herself—and with Jacob. It seemed Jacob had adopted her into his family by the time spring was arriving.

The three of them had begun to do things, much like a family would do together. There were trips to the zoo, back yard kick ball, and dinners out together. Becca had begun to attend pre-school programs and baking cupcakes for birthday parties for Jacob's friends.

Every Sunday morning, Jacob would sit beside Becca and nestle himself under her arm when he became tired from sitting.

There was definitely a perfect friendship between herself and Arron, but the bond she felt with Jacob was undeniable.

Aaron had confided in her that there was no one left to take care of Jacob should anything happen to himself. His father was ill and not capable to take Jacob in. He had a grandmother who was well along in years and she too would not be able to care for Jacob.

Aaron knew Jacob needed a mother figure in his life to help Jacob with the things that mothers are best at. He often talked about his wife wanting to make sure that Jacob was raised in a godly manner.

Becca could tell by the way that Aaron talked about his wife that he loved her very much and missed her every day. She also could tell by the way he was with Jacob that he loved him as much as he missed his wife.

Becca cherished the time she had shared with Aaron just talking and was thankful that God had allowed him to share things with her that he hadn't shared with anyone else.

She knew it was time to share with Aaron the one thing she had never shared with anyone else either. She knew she could trust him to not judge her. She would wait until the right time and she asked God to prepare that time for her when he knew she was ready for it.

Becca thought that part of the closeness she felt with Aaron resulted from her admiring how Aaron and his wife had adopted a child.

She felt she could trust Aaron and that trust grew day by day. Finally, she decided to open up and share her deepest secret with him. He had shared memories of his wife, memories of his childhood and had painfully shared some of the mistakes he had made—in both his personal life and relationships.

Aaron had grown up without a father and had experienced the pain of "something missing" just as she had suffered by not having a mother while she was growing up.

The next night, Jacob had gone to bed a little earlier than usual. Becca had prepared a homemade chocolate pie for herself and Aaron to share when he got home from work. It was almost as if Aaron knew that she needed him not to dominate the conversation that evening.

Aaron told Becca about his day and got caught up on Jacob's day. Then sat silently while watching the traffic pass by.

The night was beautiful. A full moon lit the porch and the crickets sang loudly during the absence of conversation. A slight breeze cooled the humid air of the stifling summer heat. The rhythm of the rocking chairs on the wooden floor played its own melody to accompany the crickets singing.

Becca silently asked God to give her the right words and phrasing to share what she had held inside for so long.

Slowly she began to speak. "Aaron, you have shared so many things with me. It makes me feel so honored you have trusted in me that way. I need to share something with you, and I know I can trust in you the same way."

Aaron turned toward her. She could tell by Aaron's expression and show of concern that she had made the right decision by putting her trust in him. She knew God had answered her prayer of giving her the opportunity she had asked and so she continued what she had started.

Chapter 18

"**I** know God's grace had saved me at this point in my life, and I am so thankful. What I am telling you goes many years back into my life. It is the reason I felt I had to start over and what lead to move here so I could do so." Becca explained, but not being able to look Aaron in the eyes.

Becca told Aaron about all the voices in her past and about the night that led her to come to Christ before she continued.

"There are other voices that filled my past life that led me to believe the opposite of the voices of that night. Voices that convinced me I was not lovable, that I was worthless. These voices convinced me that more than anything I was a burden."

Becca cleared her throat and dried her eyes before speaking again.

"All the relationships I have ever been in, led to someone walking out and leaving—just giving up on everything. The story and reasons were always the same. I spent all my live, energy and time encouraging others to pursue their dreams and desires. I worked when I had work and all the while I spent a great deal of time pouring myself into what was important to someone else.

In the end it was as if none of that mattered. None of it was important enough or appreciated enough. I wasted my whole life, until now, giving up on my dreams to put others needs first. I know God has used these things in my past to give me strength. I know now that someday I will see the purpose God has in all this."

Becca paused again to take a few deep breaths. Then she continued.

"It is hard to have any self confidence when no matter how hard you try you are bombarded with words like; you don't satisfy me, you just can't make me happy, you don't do enough to help me, you're not attractive enough for me or you don't fulfill my personal desires."

"I have learned that and now understand that all these things I have been told are not truth. I have come to understand that it wasn't *all* me or my short comings that caused these relationships not to last. I know that deep down inside of me that no matter how tough times get and no matter what the problem is, it is one's dedication to the commitment that makes a relationship work. I would have never left any of these relationships and I never did. Don't' get me wrong. I had my share of problems to deal with inside of myself. But, the one thing I do know about myself is that once I make a commitment, I stick to it. I just want so badly, even now, for someone to do the same for me."

"Each time a relationship didn't last, a little piece of me died. This leads me to the event that I have hid from everyone."

"Ten years ago, I was married to *him*. His name isn't important. Even to this day, it is hard for me to hear his name, even when I am saying it. I guess you could say that in the beginning, he was everything I thought I wanted. Truth be known, I now understand he really wasn't."

"He was outgoing and outspoken. He was sure of himself in everything he did. I never saw anything he set out to do, that he wasn't able to do. And he did it to perfection."

"The first two years we were together, before we were married we separated five or six times. It was so frequent, I lost count. I always figured it was because deep down inside, he really didn't know what he really wanted."

"Finally, we got married and the first couple of years of the marriage were wonderful. We did everything together. He seemed to be proud to have me by his side. He constantly bragged on me—how I was a good wife."

"Shortly into the third year, he grew more and more discontent. He had less and less time to spend with me. I guess I started pulling away, too, at that point. Mainly because I knew what would be coming. I was resentful because I could see it happening right in front of my eyes and there wasn't anything I could do about it. The situation seemed like a snowball barreling down a mountain side. Once it started, there was no stopping it."

"Eventually, after months of threatening to tear what remained apart, he left. After he left, I found myself being content and finding myself again. The whole process made me realize what was important to me once more. It taught me what I really wanted in a relationship. What I really wanted was nothing like what I had thought. I learned that I want someone to share the hard times with, someone to enjoy the good times with. I want someone to encourage me and for me to encourage them just as much. I want someone to uplift and edify and vice versa. I want someone to overlook my short comings because of the love they feel for me is so much stronger than my weaknesses. I want a relationship where we both put the other first, before ourselves—except for God. He needs to come first. I guess you could say that I feel that whoever I am in a relationship with, if he truly puts God first, then I can have all confidence that they will treat our relationship as God wants it to be treated—he will be there for me as Christ is for the church."

Becca stopped to take a break. She got herself and Aaron another glass of iced tea and returned to the porch where Aaron sat waiting patiently. Aaron's patience made her anxious to continue her story. Her fear of telling Aaron was all but gone.

"Two years later after he left, when I met someone else. I thought he had all the qualities that I admired. It seemed as though he had all the thoughts about relationships that I just shared with you that are important to me now."

"For a long while, he put me first and was determined that I knew where I stood with him. He made me his top priority. He would call during the day, just to say I love you and ask me how my day was going. There was lots of attention and compliments, just as in the previous relationship."

"Needless to say, because I was not accustomed to being treated that way, I didn't trust in him enough to accept his actions and words as truth. Over time that changed. I started believing in him and developed complete confidence in his feelings for me and our relationship. I confess that there were moments of lapse. Something that was said or an action brought all those horrible things back to me that told me no one like him could ever really love me. After those feelings subsided, it was like I had to start all over again to trust and believe in him."

"I knew I was a good person. I knew I was caring, kind, loving, compassionate, committed, trust worthy and loyal. I knew I deserved better than I had gotten from relationships in my past. I wish I had realized back then that when you think you deserve something so much, you don't appreciate it when you get it. You can't see or acknowledge the goodness and love you are shown from another because you are blinded in thinking it was because of you. You think it was because of something you had done, or the way you are that gained you those things. If only I had seen that I really didn't deserve those things. Although I possessed such wonderful qualities, the other qualities I possessed like; selfishness, pride, jealousy, skepticism and unbelief brought me back to a place of being undeserving."

"I learned things though out this time of struggle. I learned that it was a continual process.

I knew it would be hard and it was hard—extremely hard, especially at first. Getting over feeling abandonment and worthlessness is one of the hardest fights I think anyone can go through. It's like an addiction. The restless feelings of thinking there is something better and the desire to find it consumes you. It leads to making such bad decisions and leads to bad behaviors that you wouldn't normally have. It takes away a piece of you a little at a time and destroys everything good in your life—to the point of finding that better thing is all that's left."

"Each battle against these feelings took all that I had within me in the beginning. Finally, there came a time in the process where one time it was just a little easier than it had been. After that the fight during those battles became less intense, then fewer and further between."

"Don't get me wrong. I still struggle from time to time with the "fight of my life", but now I know who I am and I recognize that when those feelings surface where they come from and who they come from. I recognize them as a lie that wants to destroy me. Now I have control over the lies instead of letting them have control over me."

"This fight took so long. I was winning. Then things changed drastically in my life. The one person who showed me that I could win the fight of pushing all the negative thoughts away I had been told about myself, abandoned me as well."

"I had given up and lost so much even in that relationship in order to be submissive to the desires of what he wanted, but in the end, it wasn't enough for him either. You see, what I didn't realize was, while I was fighting my battle, he too was fighting his own demons and losing. He never told me until it was too late."

"At that point he was so unhappy with himself and me, I found myself willing to do almost anything to save our relationship. I had just found out I was pregnant. Needless to say, he didn't want a child at that point in his life. He explained that keeping the child would result in him walking away from what we had. I agreed, at that point in time, to give the child up for adoption. I convinced myself I was doing what I had to do and was willing to sacrifice everything for him."

"Two weeks after signing the papers to give up my child, he walked out anyway."

"I have tried hard to bury this secret deep inside in an attempt to hide it even from myself but it haunts me day and night. Not telling anyone about it had made the burden heavier. I know God has forgiven me for this mistake, and all my other mistakes as well, but I felt that somehow He wanted me to share this with you. Maybe because it was someone just like you who adopted my child and gave him a loving and stable home."

"I trusted you enough not to judge me harshly because of your experience with Jacob."

"I have found peace and now believe that God has placed my son with a wonderful parent like you. But, it's still my deepest regret that I will never know him, never hear his laughter, never care for him when he is sick, never be able to . . ."

Becca had to stop. The emotions were too overwhelming to continue.

Aaron leaned over to Becca and held her until she regained her composure. He laid his fingers on her cheek, turning her face toward him. He looked her directly in the eyes and began to speak.

"Becca, I have secrets, too. When the time is right, I will share them with you as well."

Chapter 19

Over the next few weeks, Becca kept eagerly awaiting Aaron sharing his secrets and struggles with her. Every evening they sat on the porch talking over a glass or fresh squeezed lemonade or sweet tea. Aaron shared stories about his mother and grandparents with her, but none of it sounded like it was something he had been hiding inside. Instead, Aaron's stories were happy. He went into much detail about his mother—her mannerisms and character. She couldn't help but get the impression that whatever his secret was that it was more of his mother's secret than his and somehow it had led to his being involved with it.

Aaron shared stories about camping trips and mischief he had gotten into in his youth. He did however share that his mother had raised him alone, without help from his father. Each time Aaron shared something with her it was similar to something she had been through. Even their likes and dislikes were strangely similar. She had never experienced that with anyone before. Most of the time, Becca felt as if she were the only person in the world who felt the way she did about certain things. It was refreshing to know she was not alone in the world with some of her deepest feelings and disappointments.

Over the next few weeks, Aaron shared things about his relationship with his wife. She could tell by looking into his eyes when he spoke about her how much he truly loved her. They had been so excited when they adopted Jacob. They joy they had felt was too indescribable to put into words, he often told her.

According to Aaron, he and his mother were saved when he was about eight years old. Up until that point, his mother had an overwhelming sadness about choices she had made in her past. After finding Christ, she was able to deal with her choices and find joy knowing that somehow God was working things out in order to bring good. When Aaron had been discouraged about not being able to see God work in the circumstances he was praying about, his mother would always remind him, "Aaron, when God works, it's hardly ever you see how He is working and what His plan is. Most of time God's working is unseen to us. It is when He is finished working and His plan is complete, is when it is revealed to us. Don't put your trust in Him by what you think you should be seeing while He is working. Put your trust in knowing that the end result is going to come. Expect to see the end result of what you have prayed for instead of desiring to see Him working to achieve it."

Becca recognized those words as something she had learned herself and smiled and nodded her head. She couldn't help but wonder what circumstances Aaron's mother had endured to have learned that lesson. She wondered if it was anything like what she had endured in her own past.

During the many talks Aaron and she had about his mother and the way he went into such detail, she could almost picture his mother's smile when something funny caught her off guard. She could see in her mind the scowl on her face when Aaron had gotten into trouble. She could feel the emotions and comfort she had felt when praying.

Somehow getting to know Aaron's mother through his stories and description of her gave her strength and encouragement in her own growth. The details Aaron gave made her feel a common bond with this woman she didn't even know. At times, she wondered how this stranger she had never met, but knew so well, would react or handle situations that Becca faced.

It never left Becca's mind that Aaron was to share his secrets with her. He seemed so transparent with her in their relationship and conversations. She couldn't imagine what he had been keeping from her all this time. Whatever it was, she knew that she would be there for him just as he had been there for her.

The end of the summer was approaching, and as every other evening, Becca and Aaron were enjoying the evening. Mrs. Kirby and the Callahan's had stopped by for a chat. During their visit, Mrs. Callahan asked Aaron is he was still playing his guitar. He commented that they hadn't heard him playing any at all as they took their afternoon stroll. He assured them he was still playing but only when he was all alone, late in the evenings. Mrs. Callahan asked if he would play just a couple of songs for her before they left.

Becca had seen the guitar leaning against the stand but it seemed like it had moved from the position it had been in for months. It hadn't crossed her mind that it belonged to Aaron. She assumed it belonged to Aaron's wife and he had left it where she had left it just as he had done with so many of her things.

Becca had asked him once about the perfume bottles and basket of yarn that he couldn't seem to put away. He had then told her that he left these things because it made him feel her presence even though she was gone.

After being gone for a few minutes, Aaron returned to the porch and began to play the most beautiful song she had ever heard played. As his fingers moved up and down the strings, she drank in the sound of each cord. She wondered how she have could have known him so well and never heard him play before.

As Aaron finished the second song for Mrs. Callahan, Jacob stepped out onto the porch.

The music had aroused him from his sleep. The Callahan's said their good-nights and headed down the street toward home.

In an effort to convince Jacob to return to bed, Aaron played a couple children's tunes on the guitar. As Jacob's eyes got heavy, Aaron began to play a melody that Becca recognized. After playing the tune through one time, Aaron began to sing the words as well.

Something began to make Becca nervous and uneasy. The song began to trigger a memory from her past but the details of where she had heard the song before refused to come. When she asked Aaron about the song, he only replied, "Mother used to sing this song at bedtime."

Chapter 20

B ecca hurried home from Bible Study. She changed from her dress clothes and slipped on something comfortable enough to throw softball with Jacob. Time that day had been hurried trying to fit in all she had to do. She had done grocery shopping for the week early in the morning. Then she stopped by the hair salon and gotten her hair trimmed before running home to put her groceries away. After a quick shower and getting dressed, she stopped by the local store to pick up something special for Jacob. Somehow she managed to make it to Bible Study just before it had begun.

This particular Bible Study was prolonged because of an unusual high volume of interaction and conversation with an abundance of comments. It was Saturday, so Becca didn't mind the study going on so long. Occasionally she had glanced at her watch, being careful about the time. She would have to leave by 12:00 to make it to Aaron's to watch Jacob the remainder of the day.

Aaron would be home by 7:00. Becca knew she wouldn't be able to stay very long talking to Aaron after he returned home that evening. She needed all the time she could find that evening to study for the Sunday school lesson she was going to teach the next morning.

Jacob was excited to see Becca, as usual. She had cut time close in arriving by noon. As she was walking in the door, Aaron had grabbed his coffee cup, kissed Jacob bye and headed quickly out the door. Becca walked behind him to the door making sure to latch the screen. As she started to turn away from the door, Aaron called her name. She stopped in her tracks and turned to look out the door.

"Becca, you know how you told me you would know when God was ready for you to share your story with me?" Aaron had slowed his pace of hurrying to leave. Before she could answer, Aaron continued, "It's time for me to share mine with you. I'll be home early, around 5:00. We'll talk then." Becca let the thought of the Sunday school lesson immediately take second place.

The rest of the day, Becca felt a nervousness that she couldn't explain. She thought maybe it was because she had waited so long for Aaron to open up to her as she had with him. She thought, too, that it would make them even closer—if that were possible.

Becca decided that she and Jacob should take advantage of their Saturday together. She packed some snacks and a blanket while Jacob grabbed the softball gloves, bat and ball. They headed to the park. Along the way, they stopped at the grill and picked up a couple of hot dogs, french fries and sodas.

Once at the park, they spread the blanket and ate their "to go" lunch. Afterwards, they threw the softball until Becca thought her arm was about to fall off. Thankfully, the Callahan's and their grandsons had the same idea about spending the day at the park.

The Callahan's told Becca how they were going to miss their afternoon walk by bringing the boys to the park. Becca assured Mr. and Mrs. Callahan she would watch all the boys, while they went for their walk. She would stay right with them and she was sure they would have fun throwing the football they had brought along with them to the park. She explained that it was a God send to her watching them and it would sure save her arm.

When the boys had gotten tired, they joined Becca on the blanket. It didn't take long for four hungry boys to devour the snacks she had brought along.

Not long afterwards, the Callahan's returned from their walk. After a short talk, she and Jacob gathered up their things and headed home in order to clean themselves up and start dinner before Aaron returned for the day.

Becca made sure Jacob had his bath while she prepared dinner. She was glad Aaron was running late. The meatloaf she was preparing had taken longer than she had expected to finish cooking.

It was 5:30 and Aaron still hadn't gotten home. Becca and Jacob decided to give it another half hour before eating without Aaron.

They covered all the food and patiently waited as they anticipated Aaron arriving shortly.

Half an hour had passed. With Aaron still not home and no phone call, Becca was beginning to worry. When Jacob walked to the table and peaked into one of the covered dishes she had fixed, Becca decided that she and Jacob should go ahead and eat. She was afraid that if she didn't follow their normal routine, Jacob would see that she was getting concerned.

Becca still hadn't heard a word out of Aaron by Jacob's bedtime. The Sunday school lesson crossed her mind, but staying with Jacob was more important. She knew she couldn't chance leaving Jacob alone—not even to run home for just a few minutes to get the material she needed to study.

Becca proceeded to get Jacob into bed. She explained to him that his father must have gotten hung up at work and would be home as soon as he could. She reassured him that she would stay as long as that would take. None the less, she could see the concern in Jacob's eyes.

Becca let Jacob pick out a book and read to him in hope that he would fall asleep quickly. She also hoped it would push away the worry she could feel within herself beginning to rise.

After finishing the book, Jacob was still awake. She badly wanted to have time to herself in order to pull herself together before Aaron returned home. Now, she felt that there was nothing left to do to get Jacob to sleep other than the one thing she had seen Aaron do when Jacob had awakened from his sleep. She began to hum the song that Aaron had played on the guitar the night they had been sitting on the porch—the one his mother sang to him as a child. As she hummed, the words strangely came easily to her as she began to sing. Before long, Jacob was sound asleep.

Becca pulled the cover up over Jacob and tucked him in, gave him a kiss on his cheek and pulled the door shut after turning off the light.

Over the next hour, Becca's mind imagined all sorts of things that could have gone wrong—an accident, a mugging, a sudden onset of illness. Aaron would have called unless something had happened that left him unable to do so. She once again made a desperate attempt to push those horrible thoughts out of her mind. She settled her mind instead on the thought that Aaron's car probably had just broken down and he was sitting on a back road waiting for someone to come along to help.

Becca had fallen asleep. She was awakened by a knock at the door. She rushed to the door to find a highway patrolman standing there with a somber look on his face. After he gave her his name and questioned her about her connection to Aaron, he asked to come inside. Becca knew immediately that her fears were not unfounded. She knew they were reality. Something horrible had happened to Aaron.

The two of them sat in the living room. Becca explained she was there taking care of Jacob while Aaron was working. The officer asked her if she could arrange to care for Jacob for the remainder of the night—until he and a social worker could return in the morning to figure out what arrangements could be made for Jacob after that. She assured the officer that she would stay and explained how much she loved Jacob.

Becca explained that she was the closest thing to family that Aaron had. And begged the officer to tell her what had happened to Aaron. Once she told him that Aaron's mother and wife were no longer living, and his father and grandmother suffered from dementia, she agreed to tell her the details of why Aaron had not returned home.

After the officer left, Becca went over and over in her mind the details of the conversation with the officer who had left just minutes ago. His words rang in her conscious. "Mr. Jackson, from what we were able to tell, was hit by a vehicle while changing a flat tire on a dark, long stretch of road between here and Wake Forest—just about twenty minutes from here. The car that hit him didn't stop. From what we can tell, death was instant, and he probably didn't even realize what had happened."

Becca appreciated the fact that he agreed to not coming back until late in the next morning. However, he requested her to see if she could locate anything in the house concerning Aaron's wishes concerning Jacob, especially since Aaron had no family to care for Jacob.

Complete devastation washed over Becca from the loss of losing the only person she had ever really felt close to.

Becca quickly realized she had to do what the officer had asked. "What will happen to Jacob if Aaron hadn't thought about this any further than he had since their last conversation about not having anyone to take of Jacob if something happened to him?" she asked herself as tears streamed down her face while thinking of losing Jacob as well as Aaron. They had become her family whom she loved deeply. She couldn't bear Jacob not being in her life.

After an hour of searching the house, Becca reluctantly went into Aaron's closet. There she found, tucked in with some insurance papers, an envelope labeled "Last Will and Testament". She opened the envelope but only found a receipt from the clerk of court for the filing of the document. She looked through the remainder of the papers Aaron had hap hazardly jumbled together, searching for a copy of the will to give to the officer in the morning. There was no sign of the will. But, at last they would know one had been filed at the court house and would be able to retrieve it on Monday.

On the top shelf, Becca noticed a small box sticking out from underneath a few articles of clothing Aaron had stacked there. She pulled it down in a last attempt to find the will. She couldn't stand thinking about Jacob being placed with strangers in the event Aaron had not left custody of Jacob to anyone Jacob already knew.

As Becca opened the box, she unfolded Aaron's birth certificate and immediately re-folded it and placed it back into the box. She thumbed through the other three or four papers that were inside the box as well. Without finding what she was looking for, she reached to replace the box where she had found it, but instead, for some reason, she slowly pulled the box back down.

Unfolding the birth certificate, once again, she began to read. Shock riddled her as she realized the contents and significance of the information she had found. As Becca read each line, unbelief and amazement left her unable to breathe. She scanned each line—County of birth, date of birth, time of birth, Mother's name, Father's name, hospital name. She couldn't believe what she was seeing as she struggled to focus on the information through the endless stream of tears that were running down her face.

After she had finally managed to finish reading Aaron's birth certificate, Becca was frozen with shock as she processed what she had just read. She returned to the living room grasping the document in her hand. She was still sitting frozen until she heard a knock at the door.

The sound of the knocking at the door jarred her from the questions she had been asking herself. Realizing it was already morning, she jumped to answer the door. It was seven o'clock in the morning. She hadn't expected the officer from last night to show up at Aaron's until later in the morning. Relief waved across her knowing she didn't have to wait longer for him to arrive.

Becca opened the door without saying a word. A social worker introduced himself. She motioned for the social worker and the officer who accompanied him to come inside. Once they had sat down, she couldn't contain herself even a second longer. "I have to run to my house and get something you must see before we discuss Jacob." Becca didn't wait for a reply from either before rushing to the door and running down the sidewalk.

Less than five minutes had passed before Becca ran back through Aaron's front door and desperately handed the officer two documents. He unfolded both. His head turned from one to the other. His mouth opened as he lifted his head and stared in disbelief at Becca. The officer slowly handed both documents to the social worker as he said, "I believe you will need this as much as I will."

He, too, examined both documents, comparing them line by line. The social worker slowly removed his glasses and took a deep breath. "I believe we have found the person who will take care of Jacob until everything can be settled permanently. Tell me, when did you discover that Mr. Jackson was your twin brother?"

Now alone in the house except for Jacob soundly sleeping in his room, Becca sat down knowing Aaron had kept his promise. He had shared his secret with her, finally. She laid the two birth certificates side by side on the table. The only difference was the time of birth. Aaron had been born five earlier than she had been born.

Becca cried as she realized that Aaron was the one who had been missing in her memories that had haunted her all those years. As the minutes passed by she realized even more—that God had allowed her get to know her brother without knowing who he was and at the same time allowed her to get to know her mother through Aaron's memories and stories about her. If she would have known the circumstances surrounding Aaron, she would have been too stubborn, still, to have allowed that to happen.

More tears flowed from Becca's eyes as Jacob walked down the hallway toward her as she embraced the fact that she was Jacob's aunt and he was her nephew.

Chapter 21

It had been eight months since Aaron's funeral. The weather had finally broke and the days were getting warm again. Becca had taken Jacob by the florist to pick up flowers to place on Aaron's grave. As, she moved away a short distance to give Jacob time to talk to Aaron, as he often did when visiting the grave, Becca's own mind was still processing how she had came to know her mother and brother and the events that had allowed that to happen since moving from the city.

Aaron had left everything he had to her so Jacob would not have to leave the home that he had been raised in thus far. Becca had only changed little things within the house since moving into Aaron's home. Most of the changes were in what was now her bedroom and in her personal bath. She couldn't see changing anything in the rest of the house since it had been perfectly decorated. She was planning on getting some minor painting done on the outside and a few pieces of wood replaced that had rotted over the winter months. Other than that, she was going to stop by the nursery and pick up some plants to place in the planters on the front porch to give some color and bring the place back to life.

Her relationship with Jacob was wonderful. It was almost unbelievable how well the two of them were getting along and coping with the situation that was new to them both. Becca, however, had been shocked a couple of months earlier when Jacob had called her "Mom" before leaving for school one morning. Since then it had become the norm for him to call her that.

Again, she was amazed how God had allowed the time she had been able to spend with Jacob and Aaron before the unforeseen events had happened, and how it had made this transition some what easier for them both.

Jacob had adjusted so well and was very happy to find out that Becca was his aunt. It had been an adjustment for Becca taking care of Jacob full-time without Aaron being there at all. But she wouldn't have had it any other way. At times, Becca found was amazed at the resemblance Jacob had to his father, in his appearance and actions. It was even more amazing seeing how many similarities Jacob seemed to have to her. She often shook her head at how God picked out the perfect family for Jacob to be adopted into.

Jacob and Becca spent every minute together that they could. Becca was going to do everything she could to ensure Jacob would never feel the aloneness she had felt growing up.

When she was alone, she would recall the talks she and Aaron had about his childhood. She was so very greatful that God allowed her to know her brother—even if for such a short time. Every time she thought about the stories Aaron had told her about their mother, and how they impacted her own life—the way she could relate to her even back then when she had no clue who she was—she knew God's grace had allowed her, in spite of her stubbornness all those years ago when her mother contacted her, to know what kind of woman her mother really was. She remembered the words Aaron once said their mother used to tell him, "Don't trust in seeing God work. Trust in the results when He is finished working." Each time she remembered her mother's saying, she smiled and was full of astonishment of how even when you don't see God working, you can be sure that when things seem to be the most difficult, He is working His hardest.

One of the most important tasks Becca had set before herself was to remind Jacob over and over again throughout her lifetime how God had worked in their lives and to encourage him as well to share their story with others.

Jacob's sixth birthday was coming up very quickly. After spending so much time with Jacob since Aaron had died, along with the time she had spent with him before that time, Becca's feelings of resentment for the son she had given away was growing by leaps and bounds. The more she had thought about it, the more she wanted to give Jacob's biological mother a gift. She wanted to find his mother, and if possible, allow her to know how wonderful Jacob was. She had no way of knowing whether or not this woman would be interested in knowing about Jacob, but she knew that she would give anything to know the child she had given up was healthy and happy.

Becca waited until Jacob was to leave for camp with the church to begin her search. Just after returning home from seeing Jacob off on the church bus, she called an attorney to see what could be done to find Jacob's mother. She made an appointment that afternoon to fill out all the paperwork and to pay for the search to get underway. While at the attorney's office, he questioned her whether or not she was sure she wanted to pursue finding this woman who had given birth to the nephew she was now raising. The attorney warned her that it could open up a can of worms that she may wish she had never opened. She assured him that she felt God had put it in her heart to find this woman and she was certain that He could handle any circumstances that arose from it.

Three days later, Becca received a phone call asking her to come to the attorney's office.

When she asked if any progress had been made, all she was told was that because of the unique circumstances of the adoption and what they had found out, it would be best if she came into the office for things to be explained to her. She sat the appointment for that afternoon.

The attorney entered the office with a look of amazement. He sat down behind his desk and flopped a folder on top of it. "Becca, this is the most amazing thing I have ever seen happen. I have handled these types of cases for fifteen years. The only thing I can say is, God does some amazing things."

Becca slid to the edge of her chair and said with excitement, "You already found her?"

The attorney raised both arms into the air and then saying, "I still can't believe this" and then lowered them placing both hands on top of the folder he had placed there and replied, "We sure did. The circumstances were so unique, the search was extremely easy. But, I have to ask you one more time if you are certain you want to know what we found out. I have no doubt this information will change your life forever!"

Becca took a deep breath and sternly said, "I am certain."

"Alright then, let's get to it. No need to put this off any longer." The attorney flipped through the file beneath his hands and pulled out some sort of document.

"Becca, this is the adoption papers your brother and sister-in-law signed when they adopted Jacob." He handed the document to her. As she was reading over the document, she hadn't seen him pull another document from the folder.

While she was still reading, he broke into the silence, "This is the document you will be wanting to see." He handed the paper to her from across his desk. "This is Jacob's original birth certificate. His biological mother's name is there as you can see."

Within seconds, Becca's eyes widened and her jaw dropped. Seconds later she look up, with her mouth still open, but wasn't able to say a word or make a sound as she tried to speak.

"That's right, Becca. I couldn't believe it either. I still can't believe it. But, it's right there in from of you." The attorney's voice got louder with excitement as he almost shouted, "**You** are Jacob's biological mother!"

Becca was overwhelmed with emotions. Tears filled her eyes—then ran down her face. She began to cry out loud. Her sobs were uncontrollable. She tried to gain her composure but was too full of wonderment, shock, and awe.

She began to pray through her tears and sobs—thanking God for restoring to her what she knew she had lost forever and would never be able to regain. She was totally broken at what God had done. She continued to cry and returned to not being able to speak.

The attorney walked over to her, laid his hand on her shoulder, handed her a box of tissues. Through his own tears, the only thing he could manage to say was, "Stay here as long as you like." Then he quietly walked from the room—closing the door behind him while drying his own tears as well.

After Becca was able to get her wits about her, she walked down the hallway, passing the attorney and his secretary. She smiled brightly and noticing the tears in both of their eyes, she stopped, looked up and said, "*My* son will be home from camp in four days."

Chapter 22

Over the next few months she realized she never had enough faith in herself to do what she had always had a passion for. She now knew that it was *not* in her own strength that things are accomplished but rather in God's strength. She had always managed to find herself involved with something because of the status it would bring her. Most of the time, whatever job she had or whatever club she had belonged to came as a result of trying to please or impress someone else.

Even when it came to her relationships, it wasn't about what she truly wanted or because they even made her happy. Life had been about getting and having. She was resolved that never again would she live that way. From now on she would live for God and the purpose He had for her.

Even though, she had everything she could have possibly wanted while living in the city, she was never content. She constantly felt like there was something missing. She never knew what it was, but she was always trying to find it. The houses, the cars, the memberships to clubs, the friends, the vacation home . . . . nothing fulfilled that void.

The only placed she had searched for contentment had been in worldly things. It had never crossed her mind that something was missing within herself—faith, belief, assurance, and knowing without a doubt that there was something better than what this world had to offer. This was the key to finding peace. All these things were found in just a few simple words, "God, forgive me for all the mistakes I have made. I have refused to listen and I've pushed you away. I have fought for control when I had none at all. *Please* come into my heart and wash me clean. Guide my steps and lift me up when I fall. Without you God, I am nothing at all. All my heart I give to you now. You are faithful and just to hear my sincere call. I am totally yours from this point on. Do with my life as you will."

Becca now had a new life, she felt more alive than she ever had. She found comfort and peace—in knowing that in her weakness she would be given strength. Finally, she totally believed that all things are possible to those who believe.

Becca was about to learn that the path of her life had lead her to be exactly where she needed to be—exactly when she needed to be there. In her heart she was praising and worshiping God with thanksgiving for waiting so patiently for her—for restoring to her the most precious thing in her life—her son.

Along the journey she had developed the passion for what she had loved so in the past—writing. She sat down at her computer and began typing, dedicating it to the One who had loved her from the beginning of time—*her* Lord and Savior. She began with these words . . . . "The night air was pleasant".